COURAGE, YOU'VE GOT IT!

Practical & Effective Self-Defense Designed by Women for Women

"In the eye of the storm, you will find courage"

By Sky M. Armstrong

www.trafford.com
North America & international
toll-free: 1 888 232 4444 (USA & Canada)
fax: 812 355 4082

Contents

PART ONE

PART TWO

PART III

ACKNOWLEDGEMENTS

Courage, You've Got It, was prepared by Sky M. Armstrong of Courage and Associates. The author thanks and would like to acknowledge the following family members, friends and experts in their fields for their generous help, encouragement, knowledge, comments and review:

To my best friend and loving husband Jack for all his support, guidance and encouragement. Thank you for tolerating all the craziness and nights of insomnia. Thank you for sharing my enthusiasm with this project and for your love and patience. I am grateful for you every day. Love you.

To my wonderful daughter Leah for the excitement and encouragement she shared with me in the making of this book. I carry you in my heart every day. I love you.

To my awesome sons, Joe and John for the many nights they prepared their own dinners and helped support me with the making of this book by being independent and self-reliant; for their encouragement to "get it done!" I love you and I am so proud of you.

To my sister, SDF, who, I hope realizes you're more than a sister to me. I've always felt lucky to have you in my life for guidance, support and love. Your humor and high sprits have always brought me out of the dark and into the sunshine. I am grateful you are a part of my life.

A special "Thanks" to a friend who came into my life at the right season, Ross A. Deck, the timing of our encounter was impeccable. Thanks for the inspiration to do it my way!

To my closest friend, Nationally known Kathylee Forrester, Children's Advocate and Founder of P.A.T.C.H.E.S (www.patcheskids.org) who has supported me through the ups and downs of this project. Thanks for holding my hand when I needed it. You have taught so many the true meaning of courage. Thanks for being the special person you are.

A special "Thank you" to a dear friend K-9 Officer Gregory S. Berry of Lancaster City Bureau of Police for assisting with the techniques within this book, assisting in the women's self-defense programs, and for offering additional input on the many questions I asked regarding the topics covered in this book.

Officer Matthew W. Brindley of Warwick Township Police Department - Identity Theft Specialist and Computer Crimes Specialist, with an additional "thank you" for giving me supplemental tips on Traveling Abroad Safety, and for assisting with the techniques within this book.

K-9 Sergeant B. Peter "Pete" Glatfelter of Lancaster City Bureau of Police

Special "Thank you" goes to a new friend K-9 Officer Jason Ziegler of Lancaster City Bureau of Police.

I would also like to thank and recognize these additional interviewees:
Sue, Sara and Jordan Glatfelter for their interview on owning dogs for protection.

A special "Thank you" to Jack R. Armstrong and Crystle Eby for their editorial review.

The biggest "Thank You" goes to a special friend who prefers to remain anonymous for editing the entire book. I feel we have been friends forever. You are highly valued here on earth particularly by me! (KLH)

A special thank you goes to all the participants that have attended the Courage and Associates women's self-defense program. A heartfelt "Thank You," to each of you, for sharing your new survival information and techniques with your female family members and friends. The knowledge you share with your loved ones will help them to realize their value. You can help with the mission to educate all females, young and old, that they do not need to tolerate abuse or be a victim of abuse. Together we can encourage and empower all females to have faith in themselves and to take charge of their future and their lives.

I would like to express my appreciation and thanks to the following friends featured in the group picture in the back of the book:

Julia A. / Crystal E. / Alicia F. / Loren D. / Richelle G. / Jacinda S. / Lisa S. / Michele T.
June K. / Megan B. / Staci B. / Jeanette S. / Taylor S. / Jordan S.

FOREWORD

Foreword By
Kathylee Forrester
Children's Advocate

"Sky Armstrong has a passionate concern for the safety of children and women. Her deep under-standing of the tricks and lures a predator would use to prey on vulnerable others should be considered knowledge any women or child should not be without. Accompany this knowledge with Sky's aware-ness programs and self-defense classes, and you create an ironclad 'prevention strategy' that I believe should be required education for all communities. It is said, God will send you an Angel in your time of need. This is exactly how I met Sky Armstrong."

In July 1994, 7-year-old Megan Kanka accepted an invitation from her neighbor in Hamilton, New Jersey to come over and see his new puppy. At the time, no one in the neighborhood was aware this man had been a twice-convicted sex offender, just waiting for the opportunity to prey upon his next victim. There of course was no puppy. After Megan entered his home, he raped and murdered her, dumping her lifeless body in a nearby park. Later, when it was realized she was missing, her murderer confirmed just what kind of monster he was by participating in the search for her body.

In August of 1994, new legislature was proposed and adopted in New Jersey called "Megan's Law," and provided community notification for neighborhoods if a sex offender was living amongst them.

My name is Kathylee Forrester. After pressing charges of rape against my own Father in 1992 and in 1993, I became an advocate and voice for children - emphasizing the need for tougher laws and prevention education. Having felt justice was served in the case of my father (being convicted and sentenced to three consecutive life terms) in August of 1994 I decided to pursue the Pennsylvania Legislature to pass Megan's Law. My life story at this point had gained national recognition, which in turn allowed Sky Armstrong to stumble across an article about me in her local paper. After reading it, she contacted me and wanted to help pursue Pennsylvania's Megan's Law. This began a 15 year friendship and passion between two women who were and are still dedicated to protecting children through awareness, confidence, education, training and life saving techniques.

Sky was an invaluable asset to me as I pursued the passage of Pennsylvania's Megan's Law. We gathered signatures for petitions, we talked to anyone who would listen and we even held a Pennsylvania's Megan's Law Rally.

Sky's passion to empower our children and women has been the drive behind her "street smart" kids and women's self-defense and awareness programs for the past several years. Her sincerity and devotion to her belief that we can teach our children life saving techniques and awareness encourages children to recognize, trust, and follow their instincts, giving them the confidence they need to speak up for themselves when in danger emotionally and or physically.

INTRODUCTION

This book addresses male against female assault, which constitutes the majority of rapes in our society. According to U.S. sexual assault 2006 statistics, 1 out of 4 women will be assaulted in their lifetime.

In 80 percent of reported rape cases, women are assaulted by someone they know. The remaining 20 percent of the reported cases are interview / blitz attacks by a stranger.

The entire contents of this book "*Courage, You've Got It*" are based upon the opinion, knowledge, training and life experiences of Sky Armstrong, unless otherwise noted.

The events shared in this book are from those participants that have taken the Courage and Associates women's self-defense program. All of their names have been withheld to protect their identity and to honor their discretion.

DISCLAIMER

Before beginning any physical, self-defense training or exercise program, get the approval of your doctor. The author, publisher, participants and distributors of this self-defense program do not assume liability for any damage or injury in connection with this self-defense program and instructions therein.

The techniques discussed in *Courage, You've Got It* are to be used if you are in fear for your life! Take the techniques seriously. They can cause temporary or permanent bodily damage possibly leading to death if executed properly.

Part One

WHAT IS THE PURPOSE OF THIS BOOK?

The purpose of this book is to educate and encourage girls and women of all ages to learn simple and effective survival techniques in an uncertain world, to heighten their awareness, and to be capable of protecting themselves against kidnapping, date rape, sexual assault, and violence towards them. This book is filled with no nonsense information that will teach the reader that you don't have to be at the mercy of criminals. It is the intention of this book to help women and girls replace fear with self-esteem and self-confidence; to give girls and women the knowledge and techniques to avoid and/ or defend themselves against date rape, being kidnapped, raped, sexually assaulted, being a victim of domestic violence or other assault situations. I want to empower every woman and girl to take charge of their future and their lives. I want all females to know they have permission to break the mold of being lady-like when someone makes them feel afraid or uncomfortable.

I want to give all of you ladies the knowledge that you have rights as a human being. No person has the right to make you feel unworthy or less than whom you really are, a Valuable person. I want to reassure you to believe in the courage you have inside yourself.

The socialization of girls begins at a very young age. Girls are taught to be nice, sweet, soft spoken and lady-like. For many of us, we were raised to not please ourselves but to please others first. Always pleasing others and never yourself robs your body of your soul. It's an old conditioning from childhood. Pleasing yourself doesn't mean you're selfish or not thoughtful of others. Pleasing yourself is healthy for you. If you don't have a healthy positive self-image you're not being all that you truly can be. Young girls and women need to know that there will be times when they must no longer be lady-like. They must be strong and aggressive. Parents need to teach their young girls to be physically aggressive and to teach them to say "NO" in an authoritive and forceful manner. Girls are raised to doubt in their own power and to think that they have to depend on men for their safety. This teaches girls to be fearful and inhibited. Girls need to be encouraged to be self-reliant and strong. If they aren't it could cost them their safety and ability to fight back when her life depends on it. I want each female to own her future and to help her take charge of her own life no matter where she is right now. We all have courage.

WHAT IS SELF-DEFENSE?

Self-defense is primarily the process of learning how to avoid being a victim. It is having the knowledge and skills to defend yourself against verbal and physical attack. Self-defense is being prepared for the unknown; it is defending oneself from attack or the threat of attack. Courage is the essence of self-defense. *Courage, You've Got It* will give you the confidence to awaken it and use it. Good self-defense is about preparedness and knowledge, not strength. Self-defense is learning to use common sense and having a good positive outlook on your everyday travels and living situations. The key to good self-defense is awareness. Exercising good judgment and using common sense can help prevent some dangers. **Unfortunately common sense is not common.**

WHO NEEDS SELF-DEFENSE?

Any person who wants to take control of their lives and future without fear needs self-defense. Don't let fear control you; control your fear and live the way you want to! This book contains no complicated holds or locks. No power punches or throws. Just very effective defense actions that can be used by a smaller person against a larger person. Self-defense is for any person who wants to take control of their own defense and future regardless of age and physical abilities. When females are uncertain and not confident in their abilities to defend themselves they are not being all they can be. Any women can feel confident and comfortable in any situation as long as they BELIEVE in themselves. Their self-defense knowledge will bring out their innermost confidence. Self-defense is not only the ability to physically defend yourself, but to verbally empower yourself; to not allow others to take advantage of you or treat you as a doormat.

The knowledge you learn in *Courage, You've Got It* will be an empowering life long skill building and enrichment program that you will use in your everyday life. The hundreds of women and girls I have taught learn self-defense exceptionally well. They become aggressive and confident in themselves and their abilities in a positive manner. Their mental attitude has gone from a helpless state to a state of self-worth, strength and self-reliance. It awakens courage they didn't realize they had. They gain confidence in their own ability to defend themselves if a situation would occur. Women and girls are realizing that they need to take responsibility for themselves.

WHY LEARN SELF-DEFENSE?

Learning self-defense helps to diminish the feeling of helplessness and panic we feel when scared or when put into an awkward position either physically or verbally. The more prepared you are to cope with situations, the less likely you are to panic. Learning self-defense helps to reduce fear. You can gain confidence to believe in yourself, know that you are a valuable person, and that your life is worth fighting for. Women and girls who learn self-defense minimize the possibility of assault and being taking advantage of, not only on the streets, but also in the work force, schools, and other areas of their everyday lives. Self-defense gives individuals inner strength and confidence so they don't hold back from trying new things. Learning self-defense teaches you to act rather than react in a situation. In self-defense you learn to use the energy of the attacker. Instead of pushing back and confronting, you redirect that energy to your advantage. In learning self-defense you will understand that strength against strength is ineffective. You'll know how to strike and where to strike. Learning self-defense does not make women less feminine; it makes them stronger individuals.

Parents: Encourage your girls to be aggressive and stand up for what they feel is right. Help them break the currently accepted definition of what constitutes feminine behavior. Allow your daughters to have a voice and to be heard. Women and girls are not helpless and should not be stereotyped as passive and helpless individuals. That is a very dangerous perception for a female. Learning self-defense can help girls be assured in their confidence and individuality.

WHO IS RESPONSIBLE FOR YOUR SAFETY?

You are! Safety is your own responsibility, which includes your work environment, traveling, being at home and in your community. The police are there to aid in your safety but your safety is up to you. By knowing self-defense techniques and by using common sense and foresight in your everyday life and travels, you can avoid trouble, allowing you to have a more stress-free life. Count on yourself for your safety.

WHAT IS RAPE?

Rape is an act of violence, aggression and hatred towards women. It is about control, not sex. Rape is a crime of forcing a female to submit to sexual intercourse. It is an act of seizing and carrying off by force. Rape is frightening, painful and emotionally scarring. It can shatter ones' spirit for a very long time and it can change who you are forever. It takes away a part of yourself.

The misconception is that rape is about sex, and not about power, control and the need to humiliate somebody. The rapist gets his rush from causing pain. Rape occurs to males and females, although women and children are the most frequent victims of this violent crime. Rape victims come from all socioeconomic and ethnic backgrounds. Victims range in age from newborns to the nineties. In this book I am referring to rape regarding a male attacking a female. Rape can take place anywhere and at any time. Eighty percent of rape is committed by someone the victim knows.

Depending on where you live, the exact definition varies, so check with your local district attorney's office to determine the statute in your state. In all 50 states the law is that rape is rape, it doesn't matter who committed the crime, your husband, a friend, a relative, a co-worker, a date or a stranger... Rape is against the law.

There are different types of rape crimes: acquaintance rape, spousal rape, rape by strangers, and incest.

Acquaintance rape is also known as date rape. Many acquaintance rapes occur in an area where the man is most familiar. This is a violent act done by someone you know such as a friend, a boyfriend, neighbor, co-worker, or a fellow student. Your risk of being raped by someone you know is four times greater than it is by a stranger. Acquaintance rape is rarely reported because few people see it as a crime punishable by law because the assault is between two people who know each other. It becomes her word against his. The woman does not always report it because the rape took place between two dating partners. They may have already had consensual sex and the violence involved was minimal. The woman feels pain, confusion, disbelief, guilt, shame, and anger and believes no one will believe her. She may feel embarrassed or ashamed about reporting the details, or because the man has a high social status and no one will believe her. Rape between people who know each other is not seduction. Rape is rape, and rape is a crime. Acquaintance rape does not just happen to college aged and older women. Classmates, boyfriends, casual friends and co-workers rape middle school and high school girls. These young teenagers do not have the knowledge and emotional strength to fight off those assaults. Mainly they fear they will be ostracized by their friends for turning in one of their own. Many of the girls deny or just won't believe it happened so they keep it to themselves, never reporting it to the police, their parents or friends. They don't see it as a real rape. These young girls could not label this assault as rape because they were not attacked by a stranger. Being assaulted by a trusted friend or boyfriend has devastating and life changing results. They may suffer inwardly for many years. They suffer from low self worth and low self esteem; their spirit has been shattered along with trust for other people, especially men. Acquaintance rape victims rarely get counseling and may consider suicide. Many never understand the true depth of this crime and the effect that it has on their life until they are much older. Sadly, many teens never tell an adult, and suffer alone for many years. Teens don't report it because of disappointing their parents; the teen may have been drinking or doing drugs or may have been with someone their parents would not approve of. There are many reasons why teens won't report a rape or get help. In my classes I have many students that will confide in me about their past and how they could never understand that what happened to them was rape, because they knew him, and couldn't believe he would betray her. The feeling of disbelief overwhelmed them. They had a hard time realizing that it was rape. They have a difficult time labeling it and realizing it was not their fault. In acquaintance rape women are more reluctant to fight, yell or run because they know the man and are mentally confused by what is going on. They're friends and she trusted him. She cannot register this in her mind at that moment as rape because he is not a stranger. Healing from the emotional ties, betrayal and deception is one of the toughest obstacles that the female will have to conquer on her own.

Women and men need to understand that being in a man's car or going to his house does not mean a woman has agreed to have sex with him. No one owes sex as a payment to anyone for dinner or an expensive time out together. Everyone has the right to say "no" to sexual activity; even if you were just kissing, no means no. Something women and men need to understand is that males and females don't physically need to have sex after becoming aroused. Men and women are still able to control themselves even after becoming aroused. Rape is about control, not sex. Most men control themselves, because most men are not rapists.

Unsafe people do not come with a warning tag, but there are signs to look out for. The following signs can help you avoid problems with future relationships. These signs are telling you that he is trying to control you and the situation, which is not a safe relationship for you to be in.

1   Refusing to hear "NO" is a clear sign of trouble in any context.

2   Belittles you either in front of friends or when alone.

3   Controls your personal environment, your hairstyle, hair color, your weight, your clothes, friends, how you should dress, etc.

4   Always chooses where to eat, what movie to see, activities to do.

5   Wants to know where you are at all times.

6   Physically grabs or pushes you.

7   Intimidates you, touches you when you tell him not to.

8   Is easily angered.

9   Doesn't treat you as an equal.

10 Enjoys bullying you, others, or animals.

11 Destroys your personal items.

12 Is rude and belittling to other women for no reason.

13 Isolates you from your family and friends.

If you notice the above traits in your relationship, you may want to consider getting out of it before you're sorry.

Sexual Assault is unwanted sexual contact between the assailant and victim. This includes touching, grabbing, fondling or using verbal sexual threats. The exact definition depends on where you live. Contact your local district attorney's office to determine the statute in your state.

Spousal rape happens to women who are married or separated from their husbands. He wants to let her know he is still in control of her. He will rape her to weaken her beliefs in her own ability to control her own life and to show her that she cannot survive without him.

Stranger rape is just as it reads. It is rape by someone you do not know.

Incestuous rape is the act of rape by a family member to another family member. This could be one's father, stepfather, uncle, grandfather, brother, cousin and so on, preying on females in the family. You can go to www.familywatchdog.us see how many sex offenders are in your area.

MIND-SET AND YOUR WILL TO WIN

Your mind-set is the most important self-defense factor for your survival. You must have mental will power to do what needs to be done to protect yourself or your loved ones. No matter what the odds are, you must fight to survive! To win at all cost you must mentally prepare yourself to use whatever force is necessary with no hesitation on your part. You must strike explosively and strike hard. You must have the will to win and the mental strength to succeed. You must believe in yourself to accomplish this goal. You can have all the training and knowledge, but without mental strength to win, the odds are against you. Begin by appreciating all that you have and plan to have in your future. The love of your family, friends, love of nature, music, laughter, fun experiences and traveling, are not things you want to lose. This strengthens your protective thinking and will help you to have a stronger mind-set on your will to win. Ask yourself, "Do you have the will to win?" You'd better. Your attacker also has the will to win, so yours must be a stronger will than his. Your attacker might take all that you love away from you. You must be a fierce fighter mentally and physically. Violence must be met with violence. The mind is a powerful element of self-defense. A confident positive mind-set is invaluable. Always be confident, alert and energetic when you are out. Pre-planning will give you added confidence if someone violates your space. It is to your advantage to know how to react prior to a confrontation. You will be scared and agitated. You will feel an adrenaline rush. This is not the time to think, "Oh, what will I do?" This is the time to know, "This is what I will do"! You must have the mind set that you can cause bodily harm to your attacker and realize that you may know him. You need to practice mentally what you will do if a confrontation does occur. The better prepared you are for a situation the less likely it is that you will panic. When scared, you will get an adrenaline rush. Use that extra energy and power to your advantage. This is not the time to think of a plan or how you will act if faced with danger because, that adrenaline rush will only last for a short time. Are you willing to use your pepper spray against an assailant even if the attacker is someone you know? Do you know how it works? Do you have it ready to use, safety switch off? Think of different types of confrontations. How are you going to act? Mentally role-play the worst-case scenarios. Role-playing is advantageous for you. Don't wait for the worst to happen; be prepared to handle it. In self-defense you must commit 100% to your survival, both mentally and physically. Do visual exercises by mentally rehearsing situations. For example, when you are watching TV or a movie and a threatening situation comes up, ask yourself, "What would I DO?" Then change your mind set to "this is what I would do if faced with that situation." It is a fact that crime is everywhere. Where you live or how you live does not guarantee your safety. Having the mind-set "it won't happen to me" is a false hope. In my classes I have taught women and girls from all walks of life. I will tell you what I tell my students. "Criminals do not care about your philosophy on life, your religion, if you're a parent or if you have a disease." Criminals only care about their own satisfaction. If they cared about you they would not be harming you. Criminals do not value you. Value yourself and defend yourself. If you can't do it for yourself, do it for your loved ones. No matter what the odds are, you must fight to survive. Be vicious and never give up. The mind and body cannot be considered separate...they must be one. You become what you put in your head. What you say to yourself matters highly and reflects on the outside to others. You either build yourself up making yourself appear strong and confident, or you tear yourself down making yourself appear weak and vulnerable. You become what you put in your head! The choice is yours and yours alone. You control what you put in your own mind and you can control how you break down what others say. Remember the saying "in one ear and out the other." Do that with all the negative remarks that people throw your way; let those negative remarks go in one ear and out the other. Purge the negative stuff you hear and fill the space with positive thoughts. Our thoughts can be our worst enemy or our ally. Process all negative viewpoints and conclusions you have about yourself and release them. Don't allow negative thoughts to rule your life. You have the power to control your thoughts. Tell your negative thoughts you choose confidence and self-belief, alter your fear of change into courage and with courage and time you will change. Say positive things to yourself just as if you were talking to a friend. Many of us give great positive advice and encouragement to others without absorbing our own good advice. At those weak times we need to practice what we preach. Change is not easy but persistence does get results.

Don't allow your present circumstances to dictate where you want to be with your life. The quality of your life is your responsibility. Your life is a gift to you. You become what you believe – if you believe you're a victim, a failure… you will be. If you believe you're a winner, a fighter, a survivor, you will be. You have to work for it. Don't allow your mind to get the better of you. If you had a hard childhood, don't let the past control your future. So many people don't enjoy the present because they allow the past to control their future. Others complain so often about life that they loss sight of what is so enjoyable about life. Instead of utilizing that negative energy for good they stay were they feel safe in the negative. Value and appreciate what you can become. Work on fulfilling what you want out of life one day at a time. We all have the power to change. It starts with a positive attitude and outlook on life. The amazing thing about life is, that we have the power to change; change is not always easy but it is not impossible. Life is full of opportunities; you have to look for them. Don't wait for opportunities to knock on your door, go knock on opportunity's door. Strive to make it happen. Never give up; you're never a failure if you give it your all! You are mentally and physically stronger than you think. <u>Don't be afraid to believe in yourself or to try something new!</u>

INTUITION

The threat of violence surrounds us every day, no matter if you live in the suburbs, the country or in the city. Crime has no limits or boundaries. Many victims of crime report they had that "bad feeling" in their gut but ignored it because they didn't want to seem rude, unfriendly or immature. They wish now that they would have been rude, unfriendly or immature. Ladies, there are times when you must put your gut feelings first and the feelings of being rude last. <u>When evil is present, your body knows.</u> Your gut feeling is known as your intuition. Intuition is the feeling of knowing something is wrong without knowing why. You have to remember what your intuition told you before you begin to analyze it. You and your intuition are connected as one. If you go against it, you will lose. Follow it and you will win. Learn to listen and trust your intuition. Intuition is a skill you can master by using it and listening and trusting in your instincts. Intuition can guide you out of trouble if you listen to it!

Check your intuition whenever you are in a high stress situation. What is your gut telling you? Trusting your intuition means tuning deep within yourself. For many of us, our intuition got pushed down at a young age. It lies asleep, waiting for us to awaken it. Now you must awaken your intuition; start to listen and trust it. This will only take a short time to learn, so start today.

Intuition is a natural survival signal that warns you of danger. No other creature in nature ignores its survival signals. Don't neglect that instinct or feeling. Being aware and alert of your surroundings at all times can help you make safer choices and act if you need to in an uncertain situation. Parents, allow your children to refuse to give hugs or kisses to people that make them feel uncomfortable. This helps your child grow confident in his or her own instincts. It gives your child a chance to know it's OK to say "no" to adults, because not all adults are safe to your child. All children want approval from their parents and forcing them to do something is not always best for the child. Children have great instincts. They are young enough to still trust and listen to their gut feelings, unlike adults who over time have programmed themselves to ignore their own instincts.

Too many people trust someone because they have a reputable position in society such as, doctors, politicians, priests, policemen, teachers, coaches, their boss, etc. They are all human. Remember that no one has the right to harm you no matter what their professional position is. Don't simply trust someone because of their rank in society, until you know exactly what their intentions are. Listen to your instincts.

Never be too shy to ask questions. Find out someone's intentions – ask "why" if you're being put in an uncomfortable position by a professional, a friend or a co-worker. If they do not have a legitimate reason or you just don't feel comfortable with their response, get yourself out of there immediately. Never worry about being rude or unfriendly, because taking this action can save your life. A good example of this is a report I was informed of by the security office of my local mall. This situation occurred three separate times at the mall parking lot. There was a teenage boy asking teenage girls as they would walk down the parking lot to help him with his car. Thank goodness these girls acted on their instincts and went back into the mall and got security. Ask yourself this…"Why would a teenage guy ask a teenage girl for automobile help." It just doesn't happen! These three girls new it wasn't right. Each one did the right thing. They turned around and went back into the mall, and then proceeded to get help. The guy immediately left the area each time and has not been caught. This situation could have become a kidnapping for those three girls. Thank God they did the right thing and listened to their gut! You can be helpful without putting yourself in danger by getting others involved.

Assault happens quickly and a lot of times we are taken off guard because we are coming to the aid of someone who is asking for our help. It is natural for most people to want to help someone in need.

Our first thought is, 'This seems innocent enough'. It doesn't seem dangerous or risky until you're in too deep to get out – so listen and trust your instincts even if it means being rude. Many people do not realize they are in trouble until they are *in trouble.* Always listen to your intuition.

LEVELS OF AWARENESS

There are different levels of awareness.

Level one is the low level. You are relaxed in the comforts of your home. You know your surroundings and sounds of your home. Your windows and doors are locked. At this level your awareness is low.

Level two is the moderate level. You leave your home to go to work or school. You will be with other people you know and you feel comfortable. At this level you should be aware of anyone new coming in your general area. Scan your surroundings knowing where all the exits are on all floors. Observe everything and everyone around you. Keep your awareness level up and your eyes open. This strengthens your senses and helps you to be alert. When going to your car be aware of who and what is around you. Have pepper spray ready. Familiarize yourself with your surroundings. Being aware can help minimize unknown surprises.

Level three is the high level. Keep alert, have pepper spray ready. You are in an unknown area.   You need to heighten your senses. Walk as though you belong there, with spirit and confidence. Never show fear or that you don't belong. If in a high crime area, take all measures that you can to make your visit there as safe as possible. Take a cab and have them wait for you if possible. Be dropped off directly in front of the building you must enter and be picked up there also. If you're walking and someone is following you, get to a well-lit, well-crowded area and get help. Never isolate yourself. Cross the street if necessary. Go into a restaurant or a store. Stay with other people until help arrives. Your plan is to deny the attacker the chance to attack you. Always take the opportunity away from your attacker, and by doing that you must always be aware of your surroundings. That is smart self-defense. At level three you will experience the fight or flight decision. Assess your situation and do what is most prudent. If you can retreat to safety, do it. If that is not possible be ready to fight. Strike hard in the target areas that you have been taught in this book. When you become aware of your environment, it enables you to increase your chances of avoiding criminal activity and confrontations. Make being aware and alert a habit in your every day life. It does not take long to make this safety measure a habit. Safety habits consist of approaching your car in a safe manner each and every time, by looking around it before you even get close to it, by checking under it and in the back seat before entering it, and locking the doors as soon as you get in. Carrying pepper spray and having it ready to use is an excellent habit. Make it a habit in your life to take measures to be safe daily. By observing people, sounds, smells and your environment, you are increasing your level of awareness, enhancing your skills, making yourself safer in your surroundings, allowing yourself to relax, and strengthening your chances of avoiding a confrontation or attack. Awareness helps you be prepared at all times. By using common sense tactics you can save yourself potential trouble. Criminals look for victims who are not aware and alert of their surroundings. Take the opportunity away from them. Your goal is to avoid being a victim of crime. Make it a habit when you enter a building, a restaurant, or a store to be aware of all exits including doors and windows, and any obstacles. By developing your level of awareness you can minimize surprise of the unknown. Many times we see only what we want to see. The reality is we should be aware and alert of our surroundings at all times. Look at things from a different perspective. Don't put caution aside, because that is when you are at risk! Be comfortable in your surroundings, but not 100% relaxed with your surroundings. The more mentally and physically prepared you are for unexpected challenges or situations, the lower your chance of being a victim.

The first defense against a surprise attack is to be alert and aware at all times.

ASSERTIVE BEHAVIOR

Assertive behavior may prevent as much as 80% of potential assaults from occurring. Walk with spirit, confidence and energy; hold your head up, shoulders back and have a bounce in your step. Gestures, body language, your attitude and tone of voice all project you as either passive or assertive. You want to project a strong self- image. You want to convey the message that you can and will take care of yourself. Always project confidence even if you have to pretend. Assertive behavior does not mean you're evil or less feminine. It means you're street smart and you are doing what you must do to protect yourself or your loved ones from danger. Don't be the victim; be the aggressor when your instincts signal danger. In a confrontation or when someone is getting in your space and your instincts are screaming "danger", use your voice as a command. Don't be afraid to be bold. Don't ask, tell! "STOP", "Back off", "Get the f--- away from me", "Get Away"", "NO", "I don't know this person and he is threatening me", "Don't touch me". Speak clearly and calmly. Using a loud voice keeps you breathing and gives you an adrenaline rush which also gives you extra strength and speed. Yelling can shock your attacker. It disrupts his plan of action and catches him off guard! Yelling also gets the attention of others, known as the 3rd person point of view. They are now your witnesses, proving you are trying to protect yourself and that you gave a verbal warning.

Raise one of your hands to shoulder height with your fingers closed and pointing up, palm facing the assailant. Do not have your hand blocking your vision. Your elbow will be bent and near your body. Stand at a 45 degree angle, 50 – 50 body weight on each foot, knees slightly bent, not locked, feet shoulder width apart. Practice this position using one of the above verbal suggested warnings.

Your tone, body language, facial expressions and your eye contact to your attacker must be in balance. Don't smile, and remain serious until the situation has deescalated and you are no longer in danger. Your aggressive action startles your attacker giving you seconds to retreat or strike explosively if needed. Most criminals do not want to get injured, nor do they want to deal with an aggressive person. They want passive weak victims; they do not want to draw attention to what they are doing. They do not want witnesses. Being verbally aggressive is to your advantage because you are getting the public involved. By using your voice you are drawing attention to the situation. When the police arrive they will be able to get more information on the assailant and know what was occurring. You need to understand that when you do something unexpected it disrupts his plan of action and catches him off guard. He now has to revise his plan mentally, allowing you seconds to retreat to safety or strike if you must. Using verbal assertiveness or physically defending yourself, no matter which you use, shows you have chosen not to be the victim. Show determination to stand your ground and protect yourself.

Don't ever show fear, panic or helplessness. This is a sign of passive behavior, telling the attacker you are an easy target, and it encourages him. You have, in unspoken words, told him you accept the role of victim and will not fight back. Passive behavior belongs to someone meek and weak-minded, and someone who can be controlled easily without a fight. Criminals look for easy targets. They will case you long before you realize you are in danger. Criminals will test you by bumping into you or by asking questions to see how you react. Are you showing signs of being afraid, uncomfortable, not looking them in the face? Or are you showing confidence, energy and strength in your verbal response. The way you respond may discourage his attempt to harm you.

Learning self-defense can help you make assertive behavior a habit in your daily life. When something is a habit, it comes naturally and instinctively to you. Make it a habit by repetition; that way you will respond instinctively when under pressure of attack. Having an assertive behavior enhances your self-confidence. Strengthen your attitude, tone, gestures and body language and see how people respond to you. You will be amazed at how people will take you seriously, and you should feel more in control of your life. Value who you are by becoming strong and confident. This will bring you a better quality of life. You no longer are in the victim role. No longer will you let others treat you as their doormat or degrade you. Believe in yourself, don't be so careful with your thoughts, be expressive, argue and cause some conflict, and own your own mind. Let yourself be heard. Don't let others manipulate you. The combination of assertive behavior and the will to win is the foundation to your success of self-defense. Assertive behavior helps you in your everyday life. You'll have better self-control, self-reliance and you will have the greatest degree of freedom from control by others. Assertive behavior parallels confidence. Confident people are less likely to be taken advantage of. Confidence permits you to fight in the face of danger. Believe in yourself and your abilities. Make it a habit to appear confident and aware even if you have to pretend you're brave. You are braver than you think!

YOUR BODY LANGUAGE

80 % of communication is your body language. The way you stand and carry yourself says a lot about you. Your posture tells others if you are feeling sad, happy, anxious, nervous, scared or confident. Your posture should move and react in a natural fluent movement. Practice aligning your center of gravity at all times. When standing in line somewhere have a 50/50 weight balance on both legs, stand at a 45 degree angle with ease of control going backward and forwards and from side to side. Have both feet facing the same direction, knees slightly bent, not locked. You should feel relaxed, yet have a keen sense of awareness of your surroundings. Your arms and hands should be relaxed. Don't fold your arms across your chest or place your hands in pockets because this restricts your reaction time. If your hands are not obstructed or confined you will have more control of yourself if a situation should occur. If someone were to bump into you, you should not lose your balance. If you do, just readjust your stance. The effectiveness in a confrontation has to do with your body language, your facial expressions, your tone of voice and your hands. You want your body to express confidence and strength. You want your voice to convey a command. You want your facial expressions to be strong and confident to the point where your attacker has to rethink his next move. Many attackers have done just that; they retreat and run, leaving the would-be victim alone. Your overall delivery will make the attacker think, "Do I really want trouble or do I want to go find someone else who is passive and weak?"

Self-defense training includes learning to recognize an aggressor and how to avoid confrontations before they begin. Sit at your local mall for about 20 minutes and observe people. You will observe confident people and meek people. You will notice people totally unaware of their surroundings and those that are aware and alert. Which do you project? The confident person walks with their chin up, shoulders straight, eyes glancing from one place to another, walking with spirit and energy with one hand free. The meek person will be looking at the ground or just focusing directly in front of themselves, never looking from side to side; they may seem stressed or rushed, shoulders shrug, chin down, and over loaded with packages leaving no hand free. To a criminal this person is an easy target because he or she appears vulnerable and is unaware. People become victims of crime because they appear vulnerable. Never concentrate so hard on something that you neglect your surroundings. Our lives are a reflection of habits that we do on a daily basis. Make it a habit to be confident and aware of your surroundings at all times. Having a non-victim response and behavior is a strong deterrent to criminals.

This is not a generalization of all rapists. The information was gathered from a group of rapists and date rapists that were interviewed. Following are characteristics a rapist may look for in a potential victim. They look at your hairstyle and often choose a woman with a ponytail, bun and long hair. Why? Because its easy to hold onto and control you.

Rapists will look at your clothing; a dress can easily be pulled up blocking your vision and controlling your arms. They look for clothes that can easily be removed. Many criminals carry scissors to cut the clothing. In his mind he will justify an attack against a women wearing a short tight fitting skirt because he views her as the women who is "asking for it". They look for women on their cell phone, digging through their purse, or women that are not aware of their surroundings as they are walking. The number one place women are abducted from or attacked is mall and grocery store parking lots.

The second place is office parking lots or garages. The third place is public restrooms.

The majority of rapists do not carry a weapon because the conviction without a weapon carries a 3 to 5 year sentence. With a weapon, the sentence is 15 to 20 years. These criminals did say that if the women put up any kind of fight, they would get discouraged because it will be time-consuming. Women carrying umbrellas in their hands or similar objects were overlooked because they could use it as a weapon. Ladies, listen to this information. It came directly from the criminals themselves. Change your habits to make yourself less of a target. Signals for your safety that we use everyday in our lives are our body language, dress, response to an event and tone of voice.

SELF-RESPECT

Self-respect is knowing you are worth defending from verbal or physical assault. It is putting a value on yourself as a person and having proper respect for oneself. Never doubt your self-worth nor sell yourself short. Self-respect leads to positive attitudes and feelings of inner peace and confidence. The phrase, "We can't love somebody else unless we love ourselves", applies here. No one will respect you or give you the respect you deserve unless you respect yourself and believe that you do deserve respect from others. You are worthy of love and respect. Be accountable for your own self-respect. Work hard at being the best you can be. A saying I enjoy is, " always be a student of life, never stop learning and keep trying to be a better person". You owe it to yourself to be the best you can be; be accountable for the decisions you make and understand the consequences of those decisions. You have the ability to control yourself mentally; you just have to decide to get rid of the negatives surrounding your life. Persevere to be the real you. Like who you are! You don't get to pick who you are but you can decide what you become. If you were a victim of any kind of abuse, you have two choices. You can submit to your abuse and to the pain and anguish and let it control your life, or you can make it work as a strength and develop courage giving you determination to rise above the pain and fear that abuse leaves you with. The pain can strengthen you and teach you more about yourself, consequently, you reveal the real you…"the you that you are proud of"

Don't be one hundred percent dependent on someone. Independence is more attractive than dependence. Never allow someone to have full control over your life. In certain classes I've noticed too many women give up their own identity for the man that supposedly loves them. Giving all control of their life to this one person allows him full control of her life. The end result is that she no longer has an identity nor accountability of herself. Her voice is never heard. Never allow anyone to have ownership over you. Own yourself because only you are accountable for you. Have the courage to stand up for yourself and have your own outspoken courage when time calls for it. You can change your way of living and circumstances by thinking positively towards your goal, one day at a time. You can overcome loneliness, financial stress or doing without material things for a period of time; it's worth the sacrifice to rid the negative that is keeping you from gaining your true self-respect. Don't let your past define who you are or who you want to be. Your worth another try, believe in yourself and just do it.

Do not allow anyone to have control over your integrity; if you loss your integrity you loss the real you. Every individual has tremendous potential and they all have blessed gifts that make them special and unique. You can't utilize or believe in those gifts if you lack self-confidence and ownership of yourself. One of our greatest blessings is the ability to change. If you are in relationships that are negative or if you are unhappy, do something about it. Follow your soul. Make your life better and change your situation; you deserve to be happy. The only person that can bring happiness in your life is you. Do not waste the precious gift of enjoying life. God wants you to prosper, to have happiness and enjoy life.

If you suffer from self-doubt, low self-esteem, or are in relationships where you are belittled by others, that negative situation holds you back from your real potential. Have the courage to change for the better, rather than dread your life. Surround yourself with people who will help you make your dreams and ambitions come true. During one of the self-defense classes at a college, one of the students shared that her boss offered to give her a raise if she would dress in a sexually provocative way. She complied with his promise for a few weeks. She enjoyed the extra money but became unhappy with herself. She expressed how she was ignored by all her fellow co-workers and how horrible and belittled she felt. Without hesitation the class began to tell her that you don't have to undress, change the way you dress for attention or for success. They joined in together sharing how all women should have respect for herself and that no amount of money or a man is worth belittling your integrity and self-respect for. In unison I heard, "never sell yourself short"! That was the first class were I didn't say a word. They said it all beautifully. The young lady of discussion quit her job the following day. During the next class together she expressed that quitting that job made her feel in-control and powerful over herself again. Her self-respect returned. There is nothing wrong with wanting to have a better way to live your life as you upgrade yourself mentally, and outwardly, appearance wise; people will learn to treat you with respect as long as you respect yourself.

We all have courage inside of us. You just need to believe in yourself and work at waking up the real you. You're there, you just need to have the courage to reach deep down inside and pull out the real you. Having self-respect and confidence in yourself is a great new journey for any person, especially for those who grew up in a bad situation. Think of it as leaving the past in the past and focusing on the new and better future. I personally know people that have broken the chains of alcoholism, drug abuse, verbal, mental, physical and sexual abuse. This type of destruction carries on from one generation to the next. Muster up the strength and courage to break the ugly patterns of destruction that gets passed down from generation to generation. The people that do break away don't posses super powers; they got to the point in their life were they knew they had to do something to stop this evil circle. Break out of that mold and never allow someone to destroy the real you!

I want to inspire females to learn more about themselves and respect being who they are. It is what you know that makes you confident in your ability to accomplish anything in your life, even in protecting yourself from danger. Learning self-defense skills will help build up your self-respect and your confidence. Have vision for your future! Be accountable for who you want to be. I have discovered that doing what you love enhances your chance for success.

Have faith in yourself; faith gives you courage. Courage allows you to believe in yourself.

Here are a few simple steps that I do daily to keep my life positive.

I stretch before I get out of bed. I eat a healthy breakfast every day. I drink a lot of water throughout my day. I try to jog in place, jump rope or do jumping jacks daily. I am always smiling; (a soft smile shows you are relaxed and approachable) I constantly focus on my posture throughout the day by sitting and standing straight. I get up from my desk and stretch every 30 minutes. I think positive thoughts and ditch negative thoughts as soon as they arrive. I keep jokes and funny pictures at my desk and look at them when the negative thoughts start coming around. I keep fruit, veggies, nuts, hot chocolate, green or black tea at my desk to snack on. I take breathe breaks when I feel stressed or rushed – breathe in and hold, let it out through your mouth!

I always listen to upbeat music to energize my attitude and myself. I try to get in touch with nature by jogging with my dog, Tank, when the weather permits. I always try to think healthy. Most important are the people I stay close to. They are my foundation. They help me be the best me I can be!

Try these suggestions and see how you feel afterwards, mentally and physically. Enjoy your life; do something just for yourself.

HOW TO USE WORDS AS A WEAPON

Verbal assertiveness can prevent eighty percent of potential assaults. Learn to use your voice as a command when a serious situation is occurring to help prevent a physical confrontation. Raise your hand at shoulder height, palm facing the attacker, fingers closed and pointing up. Be forceful and clear. Your tone conveys the message that you refuse to be a victim. Yelling awakens your survival instinct. It keeps you breathing and gives you an adrenaline rush. Yelling helps women shorten the freeze response when in a dangerous situation. Yelling is an unexpected behavior and a startling action giving you seconds to retreat or strike explosively. Forceful words catch your attacker off guard and disrupts his plan of action. Words can be used as a weapon. Practice saying, STOP", "Back off", "Get the f--- away from me", "Get Away"', "NO", "I don't know this person he is threatening me", "Don't touch me". You must practice to get comfortable with hearing yourself in an assertive behavior. Practice in your car, bathroom, in front of a mirror or in a closet. Be sure to tell your family members what you are doing, or better yet, have them join you. Don't be embarrassed, nor worry about being rude. Verbal assertive behavior is a great first defense from a threat. Your tone of voice conveys your real attitude towards your attacker. Let him know you are not going to be a willing victim and you are going to fight with all your might.

Practice yelling some of the suggested commands listed above in a forceful clear voice and look serious. Raise your hand as described above and add a small step forward. This is an advanced assertive behavior telling your attacker that you are going to fight and fight hard.

CONFRONTATIONS

It may seem easy to ignore a stranger to avoid a confrontation, but not in all situations, because the other person may be mentally deranged, on drugs or under the influence of alcohol. In this situation the safest thing to do is remove yourself from that location. Leave the area at once and call the police if necessary. The best way to avoid confrontation with a stranger is to always be aware of what is going on around you. Know where a safe place is if you need to dart into one. Know who is around and be aware of their behavior. If their behavior seems odd, it's best to remove yourself from that area. Don't be shocked by someone else's rudeness or vulgarity. They will feed off your disgust and become more vulgar. It is best to ignore them and walk away.

Listen to what noises are coming from behind you as well as in front of you. Many times you can sense trouble and you will know what route to take next. If sitting at an outside restaurant table and you pick up on violent angry voices behind you, chances are that situation could turn ugly quickly. Be sure to keep your radar up and look for an easy path leading out to a safe location. Never be so caught up in your own situation that you miss what is going on around you.

When dealing with a co-worker, spouse or child, try putting yourself in their shoes. You want to avoid belittling their pride. Empathy helps all parties involved. We all want to be heard, we all want to save face and we all at many times just don't communicate clearly what we are really trying to say. When you disrespect someone's feelings, you lose power with them. You want both parties to feel as they have been heard and then it will be a win – win situation. Communicate clearly.

In an argument, paraphrase what that person just said to you so he or she knows what you heard and if there was something left out. To diffuse a confrontation at home or at work when you just can't come to an agreement, use dialogue to lessen the situation and allow everyone involved time to collect rational thoughts and calm any hostile situations that might occur.

Try saying, "I am being as reasonable as I know how. I just see it differently than you. Can you give me some time to rethink the situation?" "I hear what you are saying and I need some time to think about it from your perspective." Another example I use is to simply say "I need time to think about it. Can I get back to you tomorrow?" "You know, your idea might work; let me think about it awhile." "That sounds great, I never thought of it like that. I will need some time and I'll get back to you in an hour." "I need to sleep on it and get back to you tomorrow!" Another example used often by someone I know is, "I heard what you said. It sounds reasonable. I need time to think more logically on that topic."

What you are trying to accomplish is for both parties to save face and lessen the tension that can come from one person feeling as though they were not heard. Assure them that you heard them by paraphrasing what they just said before you leave the room. Leaving it at that gives you both a reasonable way out and it leaves the other person feeling worthy, allowing all involved to step aside with no one looking foolish or embarrassed.

If someone is bullying you let him or her know about it up front. Let the person know that this is making you feel humiliated. Say, "I don't like it when you (fill in with the act they are doing). I wish you would stop." They may not have realized how far they went, or they said it out of frustration or immaturity, and you need to speak up for yourself. When they realize they hurt you personally, they may offer an apology and try to make things right again. Always control your own anger and don't get emotional. Showing emotion only weakens you. If you lose your composure to anger you will lose control of your rational thinking and control of your self-defense techniques. Staying calm and thinking objectively is the best way to defuse a situation and get out safely. When confronting this person maintain eye contact, relax your face and body. Have a 50 – 50 body weight on each foot, knees slightly bent, not locked, feet shoulder width apart. Hands in front or to your side. Do not cross your arms or legs. Do not step into their personal space. Express yourself in a calm, clear tone.

Let's address confrontation with a stranger. If someone has locked eyes on you, ignore him or her. Do not become hostile and do not give a smart comment back if asked, "What are you looking at?" Simply say, "Excuse me, I thought you were someone else." Be friendly. It does not matter what they think. You could also respond with "Do you work nearby? You look familiar." Use dialogue to lessen the situation so both parties save face. "Nice day, isn't it?" Make a simple statement and then ask them a question. This changes their opinion of you from hostile to friendly. Something I use is, "I was admiring your watch (or necklace). It looks very unique." This approach compliments them and calms down a confrontation that could have become ugly.

THE CRIMINAL MIND

Criminals have no limits, nor do they care about your philosophy on life, your religion or if you are a parent. Your life is insignificant to them. Your assailant is only concerned about his own desires and impulses. People do not come with a warning tag, stating "danger". Criminals can make themselves blend in with others. They can appear friendly, innocent, nice and charming. In an interview of a high profile serial rapist and murderer, he was asked how he selected his victims. These were his words; "I selected my targets based on whether they were alert and aware of their environment. If they were alert and aware I would look for someone else." This serial rapist and murderer dehumanized his victims and cased them without their knowledge. Always be alert and aware of your surroundings. Appear confident when you are out. These simple measures can save your life. Believe in your ability to defend yourself and always value yourself. No matter what the odds are, you must fight to survive. Be vicious and never give up. Never let fear stand in your way! Do not let the size or strength of a man intimidate you! Spirit and attitude are more important than size and strength.

I have seen some disturbing filmed interviews with convicted rapists. Most of the rapists believed all women to be passive and helpless. They chose the women that walked with their heads down, not looking around, because they were easy targets. They passed up women that appeared to be confident and aware of their surroundings. I noticed also that criminals weed out the weak, just as they see niceness as weakness in women. Many criminals look for an opportunity, so take that opportunity away from them. Studies also show a percentage of sexual assault is prevented by the women being aggressive and having the will to fight. Don't think that being submissive will keep you from injury or death. Fight for your virtue, for your survival, and those that love you.

Don't take everything at face value. Criminals will play on your sympathy. Don't be sympathetic, it may get you raped or killed. Always be suspicious if someone is asking "for help." Ted Bundy, the serial rapist and killer, pretended to be hurt to play on women's sympathy. If someone is asking for your help it is okay to be rude for your own safety. Tell them you will call the police to assist them or go back to the store and get a security guard. Always be on guard and ask yourself, "Why does this person need my help?" In my classes I have had women tell me that they where approached by a man asking them to help with their car, just like the three teenage girls at the mall parking lot. Think about that. First, how many women do you know who are mechanically inclined about vehicles? Not many. Second, how many men are really going to ask a woman for automobile help? It goes against the male ego. Again ask yourself "Why, does this person want my help"? The act of politeness could cost you your life. You can be helpful by getting others involved. Don't jeopardize your own safety. Never put your safety in danger just for the sake of being polite. I would rather be rude and safe and have that person complaining about my rudeness, than having my loved ones put my picture on the 6 o'clock news as a missing person. Your safety always comes first. It is OKAY to be rude.

FIGHT OR FLIGHT

What is your course of action in a fearful situation? Fight or flight? This is up to every individual. You must decide to fight to survive or run to safety if possible. If you choose to fight you must choose to break all the rules to win. You must be explosive with your strikes with no hesitation on your part. You must be willing to finish the job once you start. You are doing what you have to do to protect yourself from harm. You must have the courage to win against all odds. If you decide to run, that is just as brave. It is a sensible way to avoid getting hurt. Retreating to safety should always be your first choice, if possible. Do report the situation to the police. The authorities need to know, and will appreciate your input of location and description of the attacker. You could very well save someone else from harm. Statistically, a very high percentage of women who fight back avoid being assaulted. The quicker your response is in defending yourself with deadly strikes, the greater your chance of escape. There is a lot of power in your decision, but you alone can make it.

FEAR

Fear is an emotion caused by real or possible danger creating a state of dread or apprehension. Fear is the realization of a threat and uncertainty. It can immobilize us, which is the goal your attacker seeks. Fear causes one to lose fine motor skills, can cause tunnel vision, and loss of hearing of what is going on around you. It causes you to hold your breath to the point of passing out, or causes you to breathe heavily. Every individual handles fear differently. Fear is what your attacker feeds on. At the same time fear is your ally. Fear is useful when understood, accepted and applied to your advantage. Understanding the way you handle fear will make you a stronger and more confident person in your own abilities. Fear jumpstarts your natural survival senses. It is your mind's way of protecting you from danger or alerting you of danger.

Fear accelerates your adrenaline, giving you extra strength and energy. Your senses of smell, sight and hearing are more in tune to your surroundings. At this point your natural fight or flight instinct kicks in. You need to be prepared to face your attacker or retreat if possible. Most importantly is learning to control your breathing. Breathe in through your nose hold for a count of 5, then release slowly through your mouth. If you do not control your breathing, chances are you will panic and pass out. So practice this breathing technique daily, whenever you are feeling excited, overwhelmed, stressed, scared or anxious. Breathing also keeps your muscles relaxed. You don't want to tighten up before you need to quickly run to safety or be too stiff to fight if necessary. Remember to yell; this action keeps you from freezing up and helps your breathing. Life is a gift and that gift can be taken away at any moment. Make the most of your life. Don't let fear control you. Control your fear and live the life you want to!

DISTRACTIONS

Distractions work to your advantage in self-defense. Distractions can be objects, your voice or body. When you behave in an unexpected manner it disrupts the attacker's plan of action and it catches him off guard, making him rethink his next move. This gives you that split second to retreat or strike explosively. If a person is coming at you in a threatening manner, use your body and voice as a distraction. In a clear, calm, forceful command, say "STOP", "Back Off", or "Get Away," as you stand sideways with your weight at a 50/50 balance, knees slightly bent, hand out at shoulder height, palm facing assailant, fingers closed and pointing upward. This is his warning.

If you are near witnesses they will see that you tried to avoid a confrontation. If the attacker continues to come toward you, you must defend yourself. Distractions are not just using words as commands but your using your body and other objects. Use objects to distract your attacker. Throw any object at your attackers face causing him to raise his hands to block the object. You can use a book, papers, cell phone, book bag, groceries, a shoe, hat, jacket, sun glasses, umbrella, hot liquid such as coffee, sticks, rocks, sand, dirt, cup or a glass, briefcase, cane, or coins. Any solid object can be used as a distraction. These items only temporarily distract your attacker, giving him temporary impairment, which gives you time to retreat to safety or strike explosively. Yell "Fire, Fire" to draw attention to your situation. Use all the means you can to deter an attack.

ITEMS TO USE AS A WEAPON

Any solid sharp object can be used to defend your self such as a pen, pencil, screwdriver, keys, etc. These solid sharp objects can be thrust into the neck, eye, groin or under the chin. Those areas can be deadly. Stabbing a solid sharp object onto the top of the hand, shoulder, solar plexus, stomach, or chest area are not as deadly but will cause pain. It may or may not shock or slow down your attacker completely. In a life-threatening situation where you are afraid for your life, you must defend yourself. I suggest striking the most sensitive areas on the body, the eyes, ears, front or side of neck, the groin and under the chin. Striking these areas may cause shock and/or death. Other items that may be used as a weapon or as a distraction in self-defense can consist of using bottles, paperweights, figurines, perfume, bug spray, household cleaners, deodorant, pesticides and disinfectant sprays, fire extinguisher, bricks, sticks, 2 x 4's, bats, golf clubs, pool cues, lamps, books, a vase, dishes, a heavy flashlight, clocks and even a telephone. Walk through your home, outdoors and in your office and look for items that you can use for your defense. Doing something is always better than doing nothing! Your best weapon is your brain. You have to keep your wits when faced with danger.

MUSCLE MEMORY

Muscle memory is practicing a technique repeatedly until it becomes second nature to you. This is also known as reflex reaction. Practicing a strike or position repeatedly locks it into your muscle memory. It is your muscle memory that kicks in when you are under stress or afraid, not your brain. As a pepper spray instructor, I naturally raise my hand in a self-defense position when I feel threatened without thinking about it. I have trained my muscle memory to kick in and it takes over. One day I was jogging and another jogger came around the same corner but from the opposite direction and it startled me. My muscle memory immediately raised my arm to fire my pepper spray without my brain realizing it. There was no hesitation on my part. The male jogger jumped back and looked shocked; it startled him completely. That is the reaction you want to get from someone. If this were an attacker I would have sprayed him fully with pepper spray allowing myself to get to a safe location. Locking your techniques into muscle memory requires you to practice repeatedly over and over. Believe me, it does not take long and it definitely is worth the time and effort. You do not want to hesitate when it comes to saving your life. You want your reactions to come naturally and immediately. To get them to act that way, you must make the time to practice. You always want to respond rather than react in a life threatening situation. You form habits at a subconscious level by repetitive actions. Self-defense training teaches you to respond to danger, not to hesitate or think about it. Muscle memory is what you will defend yourself with, not your mind.

JUSTIFICATION

In my state of Pennsylvania I got a copy of the general principles of justification from the local courthouse. In the state of Pennsylvania, Chapter 5 – Title 18, 18 Pa CS 505 reads, "use of deadly force in self-protection is allowed if the person is in fear of their life." Check with your local police or go to the courthouse and get a copy for your own records.

Know what your rights are. If you are in imminent danger of serious injury or death you must use deadly force to protect yourself.

PEPPER SPRAY

Pepper spray is an amazing item that you can carry with you almost anywhere. It is inexpensive, compact and very effective on an assailant. It allows you to protect yourself from an assault and retreat to safety. It is a wonderful item that carries a powerful punch. Pepper spray is 100 percent natural. It is made of hot peppers and corn oil. It is a highly concentrated derivative of oleoresin capsicum. In more than 30 years of use by police and civilians there has never been a single substantiated case of lasting health damage caused by pepper spray.

You are NOT permitted to take it on-board planes, neither on you nor in your carry-on luggage. Do not bring it into a government building, a school or a hospital. It will be confiscated and you could get yourself in legal trouble.

Like all aerosols, pepper spray works only right side up and may lose pressure over time. Never carry a spray canister for more than one year. Get yourself a new one annually and use the old spray for target practice. Be sure you are outdoors and spray down wind, away from people and pets.

Take it along when you go camping, hiking, to outdoor events… and keep it with you. If an animal attacks, defend your self and loved ones by spraying the animal in the face, then retreat. Pepper spray will not cause harm to an animal. When threatened, your first response should be spray and retreat to safety. Don't carry pepper spray as if it were some sort of good-luck charm. Test it so you know HOW it works and confirm that it works. Do this by spraying down wind, away from people and pets. Test your unit by doing a quick one-second burst. If the spray seems weak or the fire range is short, replace it. If there is build up on the nozzle, run it under warm water. If you do use your pepper spray in a protective manner, replace it immediately. You do not know how much spray is left in the unit. Pepper spray comes out as a liquid and stays liquid when it hits. The liquid spray penetrates the attacker's skin pores and mucous membranes. The spray is absorbed into the mucus membranes causing impaired vision; the eyes will seal with tears and the nose will run. Excessive coughing to a gagging feeling, a burning sensation to the skin and lungs, and shortness of breath will occur. It can render your attacker helpless. Many pepper sprays have a marking dye in the spray to easily identify the attacker. The most effective shooting range is from an extremely close encounter to ten feet away from your attacker. The effect of pepper spray lasts from 20 to 90 minutes depending on how much you sprayed.

Do not leave pepper spray in a vehicle when it is hot outdoors because the unit could possibly explode. Look for the designated vehicle safe pepper spray.

The types of spray patterns to look for are a cone mist style or stream pattern. The stream style is good for a longer distance. The one I recommend is the cone mist style because it is better for close range shooting. Most physical assaults are a close encounter. Both types are effective. Try to shoot at the face so when the attacker inhales air he will be inhaling the O.C., causing the effects to react immediately. Once you fired on the assailant do not stay in that location. Get to a well-lit populated area and call the police immediately.

HOW TO USE YOUR PEPPER SPRAY - When a potential threat presents itself, execute your pepper spray at the last moment and spray directly at your attacker's upper body. <u>Do not announce,</u> "I have pepper spray and I will use it"! Aim the spray at the assailant and just shoot. The element of surprise is to your advantage.

I TEACH MY STUDENTS IN THIS MANNER - Hold your pepper spray and aim towards the upper body. As you spray your assailant, step out to the side and continue spraying the attacker. You will spray in a tight, small circular motion. Hold your breath for a few seconds. This is to avoid inhaling any blow-back, and stepping to the side gets you out of the last visual location that he saw you in. Your assailant may hold his breath, close his eyes and rush you in the last place he saw you. So to avoid getting tackled, get out of his path. You must practice using your pepper spray because the units are different in size, the safety mechanism is positioned differently on units and depending where you keep your pepper spray you must be able to access it with ease. Clip your pepper spray on the side of your purse. Don't allow it to settle on the bottom. You won't have enough time to retrieve it quickly and be able to use it against an attack in an appropriate amount of time. It would be to late! Practice getting your pepper spray out of your purse quickly, and know where the safety mechanism is. Get familiar with the pepper spray unit because it can save your life.

If confronted by an assailant with a gun, do not use your pepper spray until he puts the weapon down. He may think that you're pulling a weapon out and he may shoot you! Wait for the opportunity to use your pepper spray. If it is a hold-up, give him the items he asks for and allow him to leave. If it turns into a sexual crime wait until he puts the gun down, and if you can retrieve your pepper spray, do so and use it. If he has a knife, keep a distance of at least 6 feet or more between you and the assailant before you spray him with your pepper spray. If you are closer, he could slash out at you and strike you with the knife. Spray as you are backing up. Do not allow the assailant to close in on you. Your most effective range is 6 to 10 feet.

If the knife or gun is pressed against your body, obviously do not use your pepper spray. Wait for the opportunity to use it when the weapon is no longer a threat. Don't rely solely on pepper spray. Learn self-defense techniques to coincide with your pepper spray defense.

For your home: Place pepper spray units in your bedroom near the bed and in all your bathrooms. Place one near your front and back door. (Out of reach of children) It is better to have these safety measures in place than have a criminal in your home and you can't retrieve your spray.

States with pepper spray restrictions include New York, Wisconsin, Massachusetts, Michigan, and California. Check with your local police department for state restrictions.

Part Two

HOME SECURITY

Your Home: Your front door is an entry way for good and bad to pass through. Whenever someone knocks at your door be alert and aware. Be alert and aware without being suspicious of everybody. Legitimate callers (UPS, postal workers, utility employees) wear uniforms, carry identification and drive commercial vehicles. Ask to see identification or phone the company to confirm their identity. Be aware of who you are opening the door to. You do not have to give a reason or excuse not to let someone in. It is your home and you are the one who decides who may or may not enter. Always know who is outside the door before you open it. If you are home alone, before you approach the door shout a man's name loudly that your getting the door. Example, "Jack, someone's at the door. I'll get it!" Then talk through the door to see who it is and what they want. Never open the door until you know who it is for certain. Have a door viewer installed and use it.

If they ask to speak to the man of the house, tell them he is working out and cannot be interrupted. You do not want to give the impression that you're home alone. If the person at the door does not take no for an answer, call 911. Never allow someone to lower your guard to open the door. For instance if someone says they have an emergency and need to use your phone, call the police for them or have them give you the number to call without opening your door. Do not let any one enter your home and do not open your door under any circumstances. You can be helpful without putting yourself and your family in danger. Some front door scams that have been used by criminals are: "My car broke down. Can I use your phone?" " I was supposed to meet your husband here to talk business; can I wait for him inside?" "Hi, my name is Jim. I am meeting your son at 4:30. I know I am early; can I wait inside?" "I am from your utility company. I need to check your unit; can I come in?" "I am interested in the house for sale up the road; could I ask you some questions about the neighborhood?" The list goes on. You can see what they are doing. The criminal is trying to lower your guard by making their stop legitimate and friendly. Do not fall for this kind of ploy. Be smart and don't open that door until you know exactly who they are and you confirm that they belong there. Make phone calls to your utility company, your husband and your kids and see if they are legit.

Do not allow your children to open the door when you're home and especially when you are not, no matter what the age or how much they fuss. Make it a rule in your family not to open the door even if you are home. Many young children feel safe opening the door knowing you are home, but you may be in another room and unaware that your child just let a stranger into your home. To stop your child from opening the door, install a lock at the top of the door. Your child must wait for a grown up to be alongside them before opening the door to anybody. Instill that in your children.

Door to door sales are often fraudulent and dangerous. They could be scanning your home for items to steal and noticing who is home and who is not. You can purchase a "No Solicitors" sign at local hardware stores. Place the sign near your front door. By law the solicitor must obey the sign or you could call the police.

On one occasion, solicitors came to my house, desperately trying to get me to open the door to see their product. I spoke through the door asking what they wanted and asked to see their solicitor's license. At that moment, they did not say a word. They immediately left...and not just my house, but the neighborhood. If you don't know who they are then don't open the door.

Secluded homes are not the only target to a criminal but all homes are a possible target. Look for weaknesses in your home and surrounding your home. Keep all your windows locked, especially the ground level windows and windows near a deck or a low roof. Most windows are not a problem for a burglar. Take the ease away from them by installing window pins or jams that are at least 5/16" diameter in every window in your home. Drill a hole through both the lower and upper window frames. Insert a long nail or window pin into the hole. You can purchase window pins at most local hardware stores. Drill a second set of holes if you wish to have the window open at times. Consider impact resistant security laminate or film for your windows.

Use timers on your lights to give the impression that someone is home. Light timers are inexpensive at hardware stores. When programming the timers, program them to come on at different times and in different rooms of your home.

Keep your entry doors locked at all times, especially your garage door. Have deadbolts installed on all entry doors. All entry doors should be 1¾ thick solid wood. Deadbolt locks should be made from hardened steel and go into the door frame by at least an inch. Use a metal strike plate and long screws. The short screws that come with most deadbolts should be replaced with long screws for added security. Your door frame should be made of hardwood or metal. Install a door viewer in your front door at your eye level. For added safety, place pepper spray close to the front door and out of the reach of children.

Notes:

1. **Deadbolts** are the best door locks to have for security. It takes a lot of power to knock in a deadbolt and makes a lot of noise. There are two types of deadbolt locks. The single cylinder design has a lever you must turn to lock and unlock which is good to have on doors that are not near windows or glass panels. A criminal can easily break the window, reach his hand in and unlock the door. The best type of deadbolt for a door that has windows or panels beside it is the double cylinder locks. This requires you to lock and unlock it with a key. Keep the key at least 5 feet from the door, keeping it out of reach to a criminal that might break a nearby window. Allow everyone in the family to know where the key is kept.

Chain locks are useless because they rip off the frame with ease and can be cut with bolt-cutters. Security bars, the kind you see in hotel rooms, are stronger and more effective, but must be installed with long screws into solid hardwood frames.

2. **Burglars** wait until no one is home or they know you are home (home invasions) to commit their crime. Keep your doors locked at all times, day and night. In some cases, criminals will call your house to see if someone is home or not. If you come home and notice your home has been burglarized do not go inside. Go to a neighbor's and call the police. If that is not an option, drive to a safe place and call the police. Do not go in your home to investigate because the criminal may still be inside. If you are inside the home when a criminal or criminals break in, leave immediately and do not stay and hide in the house. Go out a door or window and call the police from a neighbor's house. If you have loved ones inside you obviously cannot leave them behind. Your first priority is to keep them safe. Be prepared by having a weapon or be ready to strike explosively and with deadly strikes. The quicker your response in defending yourself and your loved ones, the greater your chance of escape. If you do

strike and incapacitate the attacker, leave the home and call the police from a neighbor's house. Do not stay in the house with the criminal, even if the criminal is unconscious.

4. The **garage door** is the largest door of your house. Keep it closed at all times. It is easy for someone to enter your garage without being seen by neighbors or being detected by yourself. Be sure your garage door opener has an uncommon code and never leave your remote in an unlocked vehicle. Your remote is just like your house key. Don't leave it unsecured.

5. **Sliding glass doors** should be secured with a bolt or pin lock. Drill a hole in the frame and the door and insert the pin. This keeps the sliding glass door in the frame, which prevents the door from being lifted out of the track. There have been reports of criminals lifting sliding glass doors right out of the track giving them complete access to your home. You could use a cut broomstick to secure a sliding glass door from being slid opened by laying the piece of wood securely in the lower track of the sliding glass door.

6. **Lights** inside and outside are a deterrent, so illuminate entrances and walkways. You can purchase screw-in light controls or a light sensor for your lights to be used inside or outside of your home at hardware stores. They turn lights on at dusk and off at dawn. They are a great addition to your safety and security. Adjust your timers to reflect your normal routine. Try to create the illusion that the house is occupied. Know the lay out of your house in the dark. Place floodlights up high so an intruder cannot unscrew the bulbs.

7. Install **motion detectors** outside of your home a light will illuminate any movement that is in the range of the motion detector.

8. Adjust **window shades** and blinds the way you would if you were home. Drawn shades can actually protect the thief as he goes through your house. Leave a radio or television on when you leave. You want to create the illusion that the house is occupied. You can purchase window blockers that allow you to see out but does not allow someone to see in. Consider security laminate or film for your window protection. Check your local hardware or auto store or in the phone book under Glass Coating and Tinting. On the internet search under security laminate.

9. Do not put your name on your **mailbox**. Use only your house number. The police, fire departments and ambulances only need to see your house number. You do not want criminals to know your or your family members names. A criminal can go up to your door and pretend to know you or another family member by just calling you by your name. He is trying to lower your guard conning you into thinking he knows you or someone else in your family. This con has gotten people hurt and robbed. Take every advantage away from criminals and keep yourself and your family safe.

10. Outside **plants** growing near your windows should always be kept trimmed low. You want to be sure no one can hide behind them. Do not have overgrown bushes or trees near walkways or doors. Keep shrubs low so no one can hide behind them. Criminals can easily hide and wait to attack you from these blind spots. Plant prickly bushes near your windows, this will discourage criminals.

Think like a criminal and case your own home. Do what needs to be done to make your castle safe.

11. **Outside your home** when gardening, getting the mail, putting out the trash, hanging the laundry or watering the lawn, be aware of your surroundings. There have been kidnappings and even attacks in people's own yards. Be prepared for the "what if" scenarios. Example: look around as you step outside get a feeling for what is going on and who is around. Don't become so focused in your outside task that you are unaware of your surroundings.

12. **Garage / Yard Sales** - Be cautious when you have a public sale. Many criminals go to these sales to scan your home for future robberies. Many innocent, kind people have allowed complete

strangers in their home to use their restroom during the garage sale. Later on the homeowner realizes they are missing items or money. Others will scope out your house casing it for a future break-in. Never allow anyone, this includes women, in your home to use your restroom or phone. Give them directions to the nearest gas station. With garage sales keep the money on your body, never place it in a box or other container that you leave unattended. Temptation will get the better of someone if you offer it. Don't be naïve. Many criminals use public sales to collect information on your home and belongings. Be smart about inviting strangers to your home.

13. **Awareness includes verbal conversations** at work, restaurants, parties, etc. Do not broadcast that you live alone or that you'll be home alone while your husband / boyfriend, or roommate is traveling. Don't publicize your vacation plans at school, work or social events. You do not know who may be overhearing your conversation and that your home will be vacant. Don't publicize dates and times of weddings, anniversaries or funerals in the local paper. Many criminals scour newspapers for notices notifying them that your home is unoccupied. Be cautious when advertising furniture, cars or other belongings in the newspaper. Use common sense. There are 2 1/2 million home invasion crimes reported a year. It only takes 6 to 8 minutes to burglarize your home.

14. Keep expensive jewelry and heirlooms in another room than the master bedroom. Be creative in your hiding place. Invest in a heavy safe for your valuables. Lightweight safes are easy to carry out, so bolt the safe to the floor.

APARTMENT SAFETY

On move-in day have all your locks changed. You never know who might still have a spare key to your new place. Have deadbolts installed on all entry doors. All entry doors should be ¾ thick solid wood. Deadbolt locks should be made from hardened steel and go into the doorframe by at least an inch. Use a metal strike plate and 3-inch screws. The short screws that come with most deadbolts you should discard and replace with long screws for added security. The longer screws reinforce the strike plate making it harder to force in the door. Your doorframes should be made of solid hardwood or metal. Install a door viewer in your front door at your eye level. Place pepper spray close to the front door where you can reach it with ease but out of reach of young children.

Deadbolts are the best door locks to have for security. It takes a lot of power to knock in a dead bolt and it makes a lot of noise. There are two types of deadbolt locks, a single cylinder design which has a lever you must turn to lock and unlock, which is good to have on doors that are not near windows or glass panels where a criminal can easily break the window and reach his hand in and unlock the door. The best type of deadbolt for a door that has windows or panels beside it is the double cylinder lock. This requires you to lock and unlock it with a key. Keep the key at least 5 feet from the door keeping it out of reach to a criminal that might break a near by window. Allow everyone in the family to know where the key is kept. Check your local building codes, they may prohibit double cylinder locks for fire safety reasons.

Chain locks are useless because they rip off the frame with ease and can be cut with bolt-cutters. Security bars, the kind hotels use, are stronger and more effective but must be installed with 3-inch long screws into solid hardwood frames.

Keep all your windows locked, especially ground level windows and windows near a deck. Most windows are not a problem for a burglar. Take the ease away from them by installing window pins or jams that are at least 5/16" diameter in every window in your apartment. Drill a hole through both the lower and upper window frames. Insert a long nail or window pin into the hole. You can purchase the pins at your local hardware store. Drill a second set of holes if you wish to have the window open at times, allowing the window to be open about 5-inches. This helps to prevent a forced entry. Consider security laminate or film for your windows.

Adjust window shades and blinds the way you would if you where home. Drawn shades can actually protect the thief as he goes through your apartment.

If you have to pay for these extra security measures it will be worth it for your peace of mind, and your landlord just might pay for half the cost. All you have to do is ask.

Work with neighbors and take appropriate measures to make hallways, stairwells, laundry and storage rooms safe. Always carry pepper spray and a flashlight in the laundry and storage rooms. I am amazed at the response I get from the students in my class that respond to the above idea of carrying pepper spray and a flash light to the laundry area. Their stories are the same. They were doing laundry and the lights went out. They screamed and most heard someone running away. Simple safety measures can help when you need it the most. Keep an extra flashlight and pepper spray unit in your laundry basket at all times. Use only your initials on your mailbox. Install a buzzer-intercom system for the main door. Pledge not to let any stranger in and have a delivery protocol that all tenants will abide too. You can form a tenant's security group with the help of your local police station.

SECURITY SYSTEMS

Security Systems for your home or apartment are a great investment as long as you use them day and night. Use your system when you are home during the day and obviously at night. There are many different types of systems such as whole house systems that are installed by security companies and that are monitored 24 hours a day, seven days a week, by that company, or the alarm is triggered to the police. Be sure to know which response the company provides before you purchase your system. Some home alarms are heard outside the house alerting neighbors who can call the police. Other systems are just heard inside your home. Be sure to know what your system offers before purchasing one. A good system will have loud sirens and possibly offer lights. You want to scare the intruder and make him think twice about entering your home.

You can purchase simple and easy-to-install alarms that you individually place on doors and windows from a hardware store. This system acts as a portable alarm and it is activated when the pull pin in the alarm system is disconnected from the base. A loud ear-piercing siren goes off and is only deactivated when you put the pin back in or the battery goes low. This is a great portable alarm to have when you travel or for college dorm rooms.

Local police departments are familiar with reputable security and alarm companies. Also check with the local Better Business Bureau.

PHONE SECURITY

Phone security is easy...simply hang up. People are taken by phone scams daily if the person on the other line is asking for donations, to participate in surveys, that you are a contest winner and they ask for personal information such as your bank account number or any bank information, credit card information, or your name and address. Hang up. Remember the saying "if it sounds too good to be true, then it probably is too good to be true." Don't be scammed!

You can call your bank or credit card companies and verify if someone tried to call you and these companies already have all that information. Never give out your bank account number or social security number. Never believe strangers on the phone, because it is the simplest way to get ripped off. If someone is rude or threatening, hang up immediately. If they call back a repeated number of times trace the call, then call the police immediately and report the situation. It is against the law to threaten someone over the phone. To trace a call, phone companies have a code. In my area it is

" * 57." Call your phone company and see what they require. Know the steps you need to take before you need to use it.

Your **answering machine** should never include your name, number or that you are not home. This is telling a criminal all the information he needs. It is also a good idea for females living alone to have a male voice on the machine. Use the word "*we*" instead of "*I am*" in your message. You want to give the impression that you do not live alone. Answering machines are great for screening calls. Use caller ID and other options. Call your phone company and get a list of available options. Criminals may call your house to see if someone is home or not.

Cell phones are great to have for emergencies in your home as well as when you're away from home. A cell phone cannot have its wires cut or have the phone taken off the hook like your home phone line can. For added security and safety, keep your cell phone charged and with you even when you're home. Find out the range of your cell phone service before you purchase it. Be sure it will work in your home as well as on your normal daily routes.

DOGS FOR PROTECTION

Another safety choice is to have a dog. Many people get a dog for companionship and believe that this new family member will have protective instincts from the minute you bring him or her home. If you don't train your dog on commands for protection purposes, your dog will not always instinctively attack when you are in danger. Yes, most dogs will develop a bond and a protective sense for their owners, but that does not mean that the dog will attack an intruder. Most dogs may bark giving a warning sign, but then may go into another room or just sniff the intruder. Dogs can sense danger and an intruder long before you can. Before you go out and get a dog for protection, you must seriously consider your options. Not all dogs are natural guard dogs no matter what breed or size; it comes down to personality and training.

A guard dog requires extensive professional training that is costly and time consuming. Remember that this dog is now part of your family and needs daily attention and care. The following are questions you need to realize and honestly ask yourself before you get a dog.

Will you have the time on a daily basis to care for your dog? If you have a family, are all parties accepting the responsibility of dog ownership? Will your dog be inside or outside of the house? There may be additional wear and tear on carpet and furniture. Do you have the money to replace these items? Do you have the room? Will you have to put up a fence? Consider all the facts of dog ownership before you go get one. Some breed of dogs have to be insured under your homeowner's insurance policy.

You will be spending less time with family members to train and care for your dog. Will they feel neglected and do you really have the extra time?

In an interview with K9 Sergeant Pete Glatfelter,expert dog handler for the City of Lancaster, PA. with his comrades K9 Officer Greg Berry and K9 Officer Jason Ziegler, they candidly shared their knowledge and experience on owning a professionally trained dog and their personal opinion of women purchasing dogs for protection.

They explained the cost and time they put into the care of their guard dog and explained the pros and cons for the average person wanting to own a trained guard dog or for someone contemplating getting a large dog, and thinking that a large dog will scare away an intruder.

My first question to the K-9 officers:

	Does having a professionally trained dog in your house make you feel safe?
Officer Greg Berry:	"Yes, it's a safety blanket for the family. A dog is a first warning device. You get advanced notice that someone is outside your home. There are times when my dog, Dak (pronounced "doc") will bark and warn us that someone is outside, but once he sees that I am up, he goes and lays down. Its like his job is over; now it's my turn."
Q:	Has the dog ever made you uncomfortable for the safety of your children?
Sergeant Glatfelter:	"No, you introduce the dog to the family in a slow manner. You want the dog to be comfortable with you as well as with your family."
Q:	How much money would you say you have spent in one year on the care for your K9 dog? (Including food, vet check up's, annual shots,)
All three officers agreed:	"Ranging from $4,000.00 to $8,000.00. That is for a trained K9 dog. The average person can expect to spend $500.00 to $1,000.00 annually for the food, chew bones, health care and shots. It all depends on the health of your dog. Dogs develop illnesses the same as people,"
Q:	What about the wear and tear on your home? Is it any different than raising kids?
Officer Greg Berry:	"We crate train the dogs from puppies. For the average person, you will find a surprise on the floor or carpet, but if you're vigilant and house train your dog with continual house training, your dog will learn where to go and where not to go. You will also learn to read your dogs signs. When you leave your dog home, put your dog in the crate," The other two officer's agreed.
Q:	How many hours in a week do you have to commit with your dog before you feel confident that he or she is trained to your commands?
Officer Jason Ziegler:	"30 minutes a day. You start with the basic obedient commands "sit", "stay", "down", "come", and work your way up to more ad-

vanced commands. You want to wait until the dog has mastered the basic commands before teaching advanced commands. Your dog has to build trust with you."

Q: How can someone find a protection dog training location?

Officer Jason Ziegler: "Call your local police department and ask the K9 Officer for referrals in your area. If your area does not have a K9 Officer, talk to local veterinarians or pet shops. The location and cost varies from state to state. Go to www.dogtraining.com and get more information. Look for a certified trainer and talk to past clients."

Q: Is it possible for an average dog owner to train his or her own dog from a book on protection dog training?

Sergeant Pete Glatfelter: "NO. You need training also. The skills that you will be taught will help you and your dog trust in each other as you train properly. Protection training is all muscle memory for your dog, the same as self-defense training is for people. You want your dog to act to the threat, not hesitate nor think about it. Muscle memory is what you will defend yourself, with not your mind. There is no room for the dog to be thinking of what he should be doing. You want that dog doing what he is supposed to do, not going out doing something else. The dog must follow your command because there is no room for error. Your training with commands will come into play when you need it."

Q: Does it matter what the age of the dog is when you begin to train your dog?

All three responded: "You should start training your dog as a puppy with the basic obedient commands "sit", "stay", "down", "heel" etc., up to 18 months. You do obedience training as well as building trust with your dog. It also depends on the physical and mental ability of the dog. At that point you will know when the dog is ready for the next step. The advanced protection training age is around 18 months to 2 years old. A 3 year old is too old for the protection training for the reasoning of the wear on the teeth and joints. When training, use words you can use with ease, because in a high stress situation, such as someone breaking into your home, you might forget certain commands. Keep it to your most comfortable language. Your dog reacts to and understands your voice and pitch. Keep in mind under stress your voice changes to a higher pitch. Your dog my not recognize your voice. You can train with hand signals along with voice commands. An example would be when you use a casual "sit" command your dog my not obey, but when you use a boisterous "SIT" you get an immediate response from the dog."

Q: Can a 5 year old dog that has just been your typical family dog become a trained protection dog?

They all agree on this one: " No", that's too old."

Q: Would you encourage most people to have a protection dog?

Officer Jason Ziegler: "No. If you want a trained dog it is going to cost a lot of money and time. You also have to have physical ability to train your dog properly. I would say get a dog for companionship and as a warning device." The other two officers agreed.

Officer Greg Berry: "You really have to invest a lot of one on one time for training," Greg commented that he spends more time with his dog than his family.

Q: In your experience as police officers, does a dog normally scare away an intruder?

Officer Jason Ziegler: "Yes, there is a large intimidation factor when you hear a dog barking. Barking also scares the criminal out of hiding and people will react to the fear of the dog, giving you that warning to act. Even an ankle bitter will alert you because the small dog is agitated and continues to bark to get your attention."

Q: I have been told how a 15 pound dog scared away an intruder trying to break into a women's home and how a large dog allowed an intruder to walk right into a person's home without giving a warning bark or becoming agitated by the stranger.

Sergeant Glatfelter: "That is true." Here again it comes down to the personality of the dog. A small dog will become agitated and wake up everyone in the house. The size does not matter. The average family dog with basic training will alert you to danger as well as a trained protection dog. It depends on the personality of your dog."

Q: Is an outside dog as effective to scare away a criminal?

Sergeant Glatfelter: "Not always. It depends on the dog's access to the property. If the criminal is in the front of the house the dog will not sense the danger. If the dog has free roam of the property, then that would be bad for the criminal." Officer Greg Berry added, "With an outside dog he may be barking his head off and as you go to open the bedroom door, there stands a criminal. That is a shock. Why take away that security while your sleeping by having your dog outside?"

Q: Is it best to have your dog inside the house for the best protection?

Sergeant Pete Glatfelter: "Yes, because you know where the dog is at all times. Your dog is your first warning device. You'd rather have the dog inside the house to protect you from the threat. You should preplan to have safety measures laid out, such as calling the police, getting everyone to a safe area, and possibly getting a weapon. Be ready to defend yourself and your family if faced with the situation. To recap, your dog is the first warning sign. Then have a plan to protect yourself and your family. Don't rely solely on your dog to keep you safe."

Q: Have there been cases where the intruder hurt the dog?

All officers agreed: "Yes, a very small percentage."

Q: Have there been cases where intruders have brought snacks for the purpose of lowering the dog's sense of danger?

Sergeant Glatfelter: "Yes, in a very small percentage, but your dog can sense danger. Here again, train your dog to only accept food from you, the handler, or a family member. Do not give your dog people food. Train your dog with a command when to eat, but even then the temptation is great for a dog not to accept food."

Q: Have intruders used pepper spray against a dog to gain enter into a home?

All officers agreed: "No, not in their experience."

Q: If someone wants to train his or her dog, what tools would you suggest?

Officer Ziegler: "Along with attending certified training courses, the electric collar (E-collar) is a great training tool. It will not cause any harm to your dog. It stimulates and tingles the skin of the dog getting the dogs attention. It startles the dog and he does not know where it is coming from." The other two officers agreed.

Q: Are veterinarians supportive of this type of training?

Officer Berry: "That all depends on the veterinarian. Most prefer the E-collar over the choker collar or prong collars, but each veterinarian has their own thought on the matter. With an e-collar you only use it for training. As soon as training is over the e-collar comes off. The benefits of the e-collar is it fine tunes bad habits.

A good example would be: Your dog is 30 feet from you and you give a command to "sit". Your dog looks at you like 'ah right". You can give the command again then use the e-collar to reinforce the command. Now he looks at you and sits immediately on command. Your dog has no idea of where that jolt comes from, that is why it works. The dog needs to know when you tell him to do something either 5 feet from you or 50 feet, he must do it on command."

You can purchase e-collars at pet shops.

If you are thinking of getting a dog you need to take the following steps to protect yourself from a lawsuit. You must stress to your veterinarian that you are training your dog to be a protection dog and you also have to notify your homeowners insurance. Find out in your state what the policy is and what does it cover. You could get sued if your dog bit the veterinarian or a neighbor. Check with your local township and ordinances about protection dogs. Your dog is your responsibility, you will be held liable.

The following interview is to help you see what concerns your children may or may not have with owning a dog.

(Sara & Jordan) Sergeant Pete Glatfelter's children:
What age were you when you got the dog? Jordan - 6 and Sara - 8

How old are you now? Sara is 19 and Jordan is 17

Q: How did you feel about having a trained K9 dog in the house at age 8?

Jordan: "I thought it was really neat. Not many dads got to bring home a tool from their job. My dad did something really special and I liked it a lot."

Sara recalled that at age 8: "It didn't really feel any different than having other dogs."

Q: Did you ever feel intimated or scared by the dog?

Jordan: "Yes, when you're 6 and you know what the dog is capable of doing, it makes you worry a little; but now as a 17 year old I think the dogs are really cool. Our dog also weighed 125 pounds. That is very intimidating to a 6 year old until you get to know him."

Sara gave an instant "No."

Q: Did the dog ever come to your rescue?

Jordan: "No, per say, but emotionally he did. If you're home alone he was like a safety blanket to me and Sara."

Sara: "In a way. Anytime that I answered the door he was always there beside me."

Q: Did the dog ever threaten a neighbor or friend that came over for a visit?

"No" replied Sara and Jordan.

Q: Where your friends afraid of your dog?

Jordan: "No, they thought he was cool." And Sara added, "Some were."

Q: Did your friends wish they had your dog?

Jordan: "Yes, on occasion."   Sara agreed.

Q: Do you consider your dog part of the family?

An immediate response from both. "Yes."

Q: What do you like most about your dog?

Jordan: "The split personality, where at work he is a trained professional and at home he is loving and relaxed. You get to grow with the dog and build a bond." Sara added, "He listened to me and not my mom. He kept the house and all of us safe."

Q: What do you like least about the dog?

Jordan: "His intimidating size when I was younger. The power is beyond comparison to a small child." Sara added, "Nothing, really."

Q: When you are living on your own, will you have a dog in your new family?

Jordan: "Yes, I plan on getting into law enforcement and getting a trained K9. A good dog is a valuable asset and a great friend for companionship and protection."

Sara: "Yes, because I have always had dogs and wouldn't know what to do without one."

The following questions were directed to Sue Glatfelter, wife of Pete, and mother of Sara and Jordan.

Q: Has the K-9 dog ever made you uncomfortable with the safety for your children?

Sue: "No"

Q: How much money would you say you have spent in one year on the care for the dog? (Including food, vet check up's, annual shots, etc.)

Sue: " I don't know – most expenses were paid for by the police department."

Q: How often did you groom and wash your dog?

Sue: "I didn't. That was Pete's responsibility."

Q: What about the wear and tear on your home... is it any different than raising kids?

Sue: "Not at all. If anything, it was probably less."

IDENTITY THEFT

Identity Theft is a crime where someone uses another person's personal information without permission such as name, address, birth date, Social Security number, bank account number or credit card number in a fraudulent manner. They do this to obtain money, merchandise, or commit other crimes. Thousands of people have their identity stolen yearly. Don't be one of them.

The best way to protect your identity is to shred everything that has your name on it. Paper shredders are not expensive and they are worth every penny. Shred junk mail, bank statements, old checks, credit card offers, credit statements, the blank checks that come with pre-approved credit cards, bank loans, pre-approved credit lines that you do not use, medical forms, copies of doctor bills, social security information and all home bills that include your name and address. A criminal can easily use this personal information and ruin your credit. Always shred the receipts you receive from gas stations and grocery stores, and never leave an ATM receipt at the bank after you made a withdrawal. Take it home, shred it, and make it a habit to shred any type of receipt or information form that has your personal information on it. When using an ATM machine protect the keypad with your hand or body keeping your PIN or password secure. Never have your PIN number on your card or carry it with you. Memorize your PIN number. You never know who may be watching and from what location. You may feel odd covering the machine when someone is behind you but your safety should take precedence over your uncomfortable feelings. It is easy for someone to steal your PIN number or password and get into your account. This simple maneuver can keep your identity safe. Take precautions when you are out. Criminals do not need all your information. The little information they do gather can go a long way to destroy your credit and identity.

Only legitimate businesses such as a bank, car dealership, or home loan lending agencies will need your bank information or Social Security number in addition to other personal information. It has been reported that store clerks have asked customers, particularly the elderly, for their Social Security number. Never give out your social security number while shopping. Stores do not require that information to make a purchase. If you are asked for bank information or your Social Security number, ask yourself "Why does this person need this?" Leave and report it to a manager. Never put your Social Security number on a check.

Never leave your vehicle registration or title lay out in your vehicle. This document has personal information on it, also. Lock it in your glove compartment or place it in a safe location in the rear of the car.

The more you do to protect all of your personal information, the lower the odds are of becoming the next victim of identity theft.

In an interview with Identity Theft Specialist; Officer Matthew W. Brindley of Warwick Township Police Department, he states that, "Identity theft is the nation's fastest growing crime right now."

He relates that to the fast paced life we live. It is the age of computers which includes on-line banking, internet purchases, and inputting personal data on electronic devises. The easy access and carelessness of individuals with their personal information makes it easy for one to fall victim to identity theft. It is not that difficult to hack into computers and access your personal information. By responding to scams over the phone, through the mail and e-mail, you fall victim to identity theft. On the rise also is dumpster diving, which is stealing mail out of mailboxes and conning information out of employees. It's the easiest way to get someone's personal information.

In an interview with Officer Brindley, he states, "It is amazing the amount of people that furnish private, confidential information to somebody over the telephone. They have no idea who they are talking to, just because someone says they are 'so and so' from 'such and such' a place. I guess they take people at their word." Never give your personal information or credit card number over the phone to someone who has called you.

Q: What is the most common way of getting someone's identity?

Officer Brindley: "That would be phishing. The criminal will steal personal information through e-mail or over the phone by posing as legitimate company personnel from your bank, mortgage company or credit card company. They will claim that there is a problem with your account and ask you for your personal information. The best advice is to ask for their phone number and go cross reference it to the number on the back of your credit card. Chances are they will hang up or curse you out, then hang up. Then you call that number on the back of your card and explain the call you just received. Call your bank or credit card where they stated they were calling from and report it. You can also verify that your account is okay. Taking safety measures into your own hands will save you a lot of nightmares and money. If you gave the imposter your personal information they will have access to all your credit accounts and bank accounts. It takes a long time to get your personal records clear. Never give out personal information to anyone over the phone or by e-mail. Don't trust someone just because they say they work for the bank or a credit card company. You do not know that for certain."

Q: To paraphrase what you are saying, "People should be their own detective and ask questions, including not taking everything at face value".

Officer Brindley: "Yes, that sums it up".

Be alert to phone scams, especially when you receive a call from a travel agency or a business that claims you have won money or a trip. If the caller asks for personal information plus your bank account number so they can transfer money into your account, take this as trouble. Once again this is a scam! What happens is, they drain your account! Again, never give out personal information. Simply hang up! As Officer Brindley puts it, "If it sounds too good to be true then it is!" Criminals can also accumulate different personal forms and collect what they need when dumpster diving. That is why it is essential to shred every piece of information that has your personal information on it.

Q: Do criminals need all your personal information?

Officer Brindley: "Criminals do not need all of your personal information to open credit cards in your name. The pre-approved credit applications you receive in the mail is all someone needs to get money. Criminals can accumulate different personal forms and collect the information needed. That is why it is important to shred all your mail that has any personal information on it. A little information can go along way with identity thieves."

Q: What exactly is dumpster diving?

Officer Brindley: "Dumpster diving is stealing mail out of your mailbox or going through your trash or business dumpsters. These acts of crime are getting national coverage. It is easy access to pre-approved applications or loans, providing thieves with personal information. Ask your doctor's office or any type business that has your personal information how they protect it and their policy on how they dispose of it."

Q: Should people have locked mailboxes?

Officer Brindley: "Any steps you take to protect your ID is a positive. This crime is the opportunity of ease; the harder you make it for someone the less likely – but there is that chance it could still happen. Nothing is 100 percent. Try to take precautions."

Q: Do criminals go to landfills to find personal data?

Officer Brindley:	"They could. It is easier for them to go to mail boxes and dumpsters, or hack into a computer system. It would be harder at a landfill. It could happen. Pretty much anywhere information can be obtained is where criminals will go!"
Q:	If a criminal gains access to your personal information, how will they use it?
Officer Brindley:	"It varies from criminal to criminal and what they stole from you - your complete personal information, your bank account number or a credit card number. The criminal will usually use it immediately to open credit cards and make purchases that cannot be traced such as gift certificates, money orders or cashiers checks. Your less intelligent criminal will mistakenly leave a trail leading back to them."
Q:	Do identity thieves use someone's personal information to get a new drivers license, birth certificate or Social Security number so they can gain your ID to cover a crime they may have committed, where you, the victim, may get arrested for it?
Officer Brindley:	"Criminals use it for false ID, yes. Since the terrorist attack they have tightened down the procedures for getting ID's. You need to provide a lot of solid information."
Q:	Is stealing wallets and purses on a rise because of easy access to personal data?
Officer Brindley:	"No, not really, because you're warned early; so it's not to the criminals advantage. They need some time to get approved or access the information and receive the new cards or checks. Usually if you lose your wallet you cancel everything right away, and if someone steals your wallet you know it immediately and cancel your cards. That is a quick response, identity theft criminals do it the anonymous way without you knowing."
Q:	Are burglars stealing personal data as well as other home items?
Officer Brindley:	"Yes, mainly checks. Secure personal information in a safe or a locked cabinet!"
Q:	What is shoulder surfing?
Officer Brindley:	"Shoulder surfing is when someone standing next to you in a checkout line memorizes your name, address and phone number. It only takes seconds. Criminals don't need all your information to destroy your good name. Be aware of who is next to you and how close they are. Keep your information safe. Write it down for the clerk, then take that piece of paper back from the clerk and shred it when you

get home. An identity thief can stand near a public phone and memorize your phone card numbers or your credit card numbers, even listen to you giving them verbally over the phone, so be observant."

Q: Do I need to give store clerks my phone number?

Officer Brindley: "No, just politely say your number is unlisted and you do not give it out!"

"A general rule is to give out what is necessary. Ask yourself why they need it. Is it relevant to my purchase? If not, then don't give it out".

Q: What is skimming and how does it work?

Officer Brindley: "Thieves steal your credit card or debt card account number at a Mac machine, a restaurant or a store by using a special data collection device called a skimmer. The card is swiped for the legitimate sale and then again through a skimmer device. The criminal may carry the skimmer device on their body or store it where he or she has easy access to it. This crime involves dishonest employees. The skimmer device can read all three tracks on your credit card and then sends it to the criminal's PC, or the criminal can e-mail the information anywhere in the world. The skimmer device can be as small as an automobile keyless entry device. Other devises look like a pager. Skimming is most likely to occur at those merchants where the card is out of the card member's sight when the sale is processed. Skimming fraud is well organized....generally international in scope. Your local law enforcement, prosecutors and technical resources are limited. Be observant with your card."

Q: Can you elaborate on that?

Officer Brindley: "You have to take the steps to protect your identity and your information. If not, you have to face the consequences – a lot of times you will get it straightened out, but it's a nightmare you are going to go through. You're going to have bad credit depending on what purchases were made. You will be dealing with collection agencies until it is all straightened out. Why make it easy for someone to commit this crime against you? Take precautions, and make it harder for someone to commit a crime against you. Protect yourself."

Q: What would you suggest people do to protect themselves from ID Theft?

Officer Brindley: "Shred everything that has your name on it. Manage your personal information safely. Never give out personal information over the phone or through the mail. Be sure to confirm that whom you are dealing with is legitimate. Check the organization's website. Many

COURAGE, YOU'VE GOT IT!

companies post scam alerts when their name was improperly used. Never leave receipts at the bank machine or gas stations, etc. Take the receipt with you and shred it when you get home. Never carry all your credit cards or a lot of cash. Never carry your Social Security card, passport or birth certificate. Do not put personal information on an electronic organizer or other devices. You never want your personal information to fall into the wrong hands. Keep copies of all your bank cards and credit cards in a locked draw or a safe. Don't use birthdays, mother's maiden name, Social Security digits or phone numbers for your password on your accounts or on your cards. They are easy to retrieve. Make it hard for someone else."

Q: Is there a national law that companies and business must follow to protect someone's ID?

Officer Brindley: "Yes, it is in process in Congress right now!"

Q: What are the signs if you're a victim of Identity Theft?

Officer Brindley: "Unexplained withdrawals or charges. You receive calls, bills or credit card statements from companies you did not open or deal with; being denied credit for no reason, any unexplained purchases (something that shows up on your account statement). Check your credit report once a year."

Q: How can someone get a free credit report?

Officer Brindley: "Go to www.annualcreditreport.com."

Q: What steps should someone take if they are a victim of Identity Theft?

Officer Brindley: "1st)   Immediately contact the 3 major credit bureaus:

     1. Equifax at www.equifax.com or call 1-800-685-1111 or 1-800-525-6285.

     2. Experian at www.experian.com or call 1-800-397-3742.

     3. Trans Union at www.transunion.com or call 1-800-916-8800 or 1-800-6807289.

You only need to call one and the other two will be notified, which puts fraud alert on your file. The fraud alert will be on your file so potential creditors know that you were a victim of Identity Theft. This may cause some delay to you in getting new credit, but it will also make it difficult for someone to get credit under your name.

2nd) Call your local police and give a report. Fill out the Identity Theft Affidavit. This is your sworn statement that you were a victim.

3rd) Close all your credit cards, bank accounts, ect.

4th) Contact all of the companies and stores ect. where fraudulent transactions took place.

5th) Call or E-mail the Federal Trade Commission to report the situation and get help from them.

FTC phone number 1-877-438-4338 or www.consumer.gov/ idtheft

FTC address is Identity Theft Clearinghouse

600 Pennsylvania Avenue

N.W., Washington DC 20580

6th) Contact The Social Security Administration fraud line at 1-800-269-027; this will help you if someone tries to open up credit.

You want to be as aggressive as possible. You do not want time to go by quickly waiting for others to help you – help yourself and be your own advocate. Go to all the Identity Theft sites on the internet and learn what to do. Keep all your originals of everything; send out copies only and use certified mail when sending out your documents to each company. You can prove that it was received. Keep a copy of everything you submit and receive. Never send originals. Keep all letters from the creditors for years stating that they closed your account and have discharged you of fraudulent debts."

Q: Is Identity Theft a federal offense?

Officer Brindley: "Yes, it is a federal crime in all 50 states. The penalty is a felony charge with maximum fines and jail time. Victims of identity theft may lose job opportunities, be refused loans, spend personal money and spend months to years clearing up their name. In most cases the victim will receive restitution. The process does not happen quickly."

(Fifty percent of Identity Theft crime occurs from someone you know, a friend, a relative, a co-worker...)

For more information on Identity Theft go to www.Identitytheft.org or www.consumer.gov/idtheft/

INTERNET SAFETY

The Internet is the world moved online. It connects you to new people, places, information, services and products you may never have had the opportunity to meet or know. The Internet also brings new dangers. You must be aware of whom you are giving information to; even the smallest amount in the wrong hands can bring you misfortune. There are some people you may meet through the Internet that want to cause you harm. The Internet itself is prone to con artists.

The Internet can provide a lot of interesting information and people. Just keep in mind that if you use your computer, you're opening the door to strangers. It is not difficult to locate your phone number or home. Unfortunately predators do abuse the Internet to get to innocent people. The Internet is the real world brought into your home and / or work place, so use it with caution. There are just as many criminals online as there are in real life. Listen to your gut. When "it does not feel right, it's not right".

In an interview with Internet Specialist; Officer Matthew W. Brindley of Warwick Township Police Department, he shared the following: "You have a lesser chance of being a victim if you would use common sense. You could avoid most problems. Every piece of information can be traced one way or another back to you, your home or place of business. Always protect your personal information and never give it out to anyone no matter how friendly they seem."

With e-mails, never respond to a pop-up...delete it immediately. Pop-ups and e-mails can cause your computer to crash by giving it a virus. Never respond to e-mails or pop-ups that ask for your personal information. Do not believe everything you read or receive by e-mail. If you do not recognize the sender, delete it. Use anti-virus software and a firewall for added security. You must update them regularly. Never e-mail personal information because e-mail is not secure. For your protection never send by e-mail your credit card number, Social Security number, birthday, tax identification number, security codes to any one or any company no matter who they say they are. Your bank, Credit Card Company and homeowners companies, will not send you an e-mail asking for your personal information. Do not send pictures over the Internet because they can be altered and used on pornography sites. Nothing on the net is 100 percent private. Many people get a false sense of security, not realizing your computer and everything you put on it is not secure or private.

Chat rooms are websites where people go to discuss topics of interest. Chat rooms can facilitate rudeness and imaginative role-play. They can contain sexual content. There are many sex criminals and predators on the web, so use caution. If someone starts asking for personal information or physical descriptions of you, log off and do not go back to that chat room. In chat rooms, many people behave differently than what they really would act like if you were meeting in person. Why are you so trusting of someone you don't know? Don't allow someone to scam you.

Teenagers should be aware of adults pretending to be a teenager. The adults will try to develop a friendship with you, then convince you to meet in person. This is extremely dangerous. It leads to physical abuse and possible abduction. Go with your gut feelings...if it doesn't feel right, its not. Leave that chat room and close down your computer. Criminals can access your home address off your computer, putting you in danger. Anyone can access public records and find your home address through public tax records or a house deed. Never use your real name or a sexual nickname in a chat room. Use a generic name or abbreviations. There is very little respect shown in chat rooms. If joining a chat room, sit for a few minutes to see the flow of the conversation before you join in. This will give you an idea of the standard allowed in that chat room. If you don't like the tone, close out. Never advertise in chat rooms that you are lonely or looking for romance...you will get obnoxious responses. Never tolerate bad manners; leave the chat room. You never really know who you are communicating with. Chat room "friends" are not always who they say they are. People you think you have come to know may say things on the Internet that they would not say or do in person. Don't take everything at face value when on the Internet, especially in chat rooms. Why are you so trusting to someone you don't know? You could be easily scammed by someone telling you exactly what you want to hear. Many criminals will con you by feeding off what information you provide. If someone wants to meet you, most times its best to say, "no". If you do meet someone, have others go with you and pick a busy restaurant to meet at. If the other person doesn't like that idea, you know you saved yourself from trouble. Be extra cautious and safe if you decide to meet someone that you met through a chat room. Common sense prevails. Just because someone says they are someone doesn't mean they are. Everyone is vulnerable to online crime, so use precautions and common sense.

When shopping online be sure it is a recognized name and a secure site. Look for httpt:// at the beginning of the web site and look for a picture of a closed lock in the bottom right corner. If the lock is not closed it is not a secure site. Call the company and ask what policy they follow to protect your personal information. Anyone can open an online store. If you're going to do business with them you should do a Google search on that company and see what comes up. Again, you're taking this information off the Internet so you do not know the source. Know what the company's return and refund policy is before you order. Get a catalog or brochure from any new company. Most sites offer customer service either by phone or E-mail. If not, take your business elsewhere. Find out your guarantee of security if you do business with that company. Check delivery dates and review the warranty. Check the Shipping and Handling cost. Know how the company secures your personal information before you do business with them. Use a password that is a combination of letters and numbers. Pay with a credit card using your credit card for online transactions; you will be protected by the Fair Credit Billing Act. If an unauthorized transaction occurs, you generally are charged $50.00. You also have the right to dispute the costs if wrongly charged. Print out and keep a record of the purchase and the confirmation number. Always ask yourself if the company needs all your personal information. Usually they don't. What the online store needs is your name, address, phone number, e-mail address and your credit card number. They do not need your birth date or social security number. If they do ask, take your business elsewhere. Protect your personal information at all cost. You do not want to be a victim of Identity theft. Only give out the information necessary to place your order and get it delivered safely to your address. Look for an online privacy policy on the web site. If it does not have one, don't take the chance of giving out personal information to an unsecured site. Look for the "opt out of" choice which you should find before your confirmation. Be sure the company has a privacy policy. This will keep your information from being shared or sold to other companies for marketing purposes. Anything you do on the computer is taking a chance. Do your best to research the company you are buying from. In the end, you have to take it for what it is. Educate yourself before you buy off the Internet; be cautious if you feel suspicious and take your business elsewhere. For more information on Internet Safety go to www.ftc.gov.

MySpace.com is a sexual predators dream and a parent's nightmare. You can get 100 or more new friends in less than a week's time by pretending to be a teenager. These predators can easily find out where you live by asking you inconspicuous questions like what school you attend, where you like to hang out, what hobbies you like, or what sports you like or play. It gives predators clues to who you are; they'll know your likes and dislikes. Soon you will feel connected to this new friend because you share the same interest. That is how predators seduce you and lower your guard, making you feel connected to them. MySpace is open to the public so don't post anything that you wouldn't want the world to know. Never post personal information of where you live, hangout, attend school, phone number, etc. People aren't always who they say they are. Report any inappropriate content to MySpace or the authorities.

If you decide to get rid of your computer you must destroy your hard drive. The only completely safe way of doing this is by soaking it in water or destroying it with a sledgehammer. If you try to wipe clean a hard drive, someone can easily bring back your information. It's not a difficult task to do.

SAFETY ON THE STREETS

Having a street-smart attitude and look can help keep you from being a victim of muggers and sexual assault. Street smarts is basic common sense. It is being aware of your surroundings at all times, knowing who is where, and what is going on. Look around to notice what shops are open or closed. Look ahead a good distance to see what's going on before you get there. Use store windows to see who is behind you. You are not being paranoid; you're using good safety precautions. Avoiding trouble is your goal.

Projecting a strong, confident self-image is wise street smarts. Walk with energy and spirit and keep your chin up, shoulders straight, eyes gazing from one place to another, and never walk looking at the ground. Keep your hands out of your pockets. If you need to respond quickly, having your hands in your pockets restricts your motion. You want to exude confidence, stating that you can handle yourself. The best defense against a surprise attack is to be alert and aware at all times. Criminals do not appear out of nowhere... they come from somewhere... the somewhere that you were not seeing. That is why it is important to be alert and aware of your surroundings.

When in unfamiliar places, pretend you belong there. Try to plan before you leave by purchasing a map of the area, and get familiar with it. Criminals look for easy targets. Take away the opportunity by not looking weak, lost or afraid. Showing fear is a sure sign of weakness to any criminal. Stay on well-traveled roads and highways and avoid back roads and so-called short cuts in unfamiliar areas. Carry a cell phone and pepper spray for your safety.

There is safety in numbers. Do not walk or jog alone at night. Many women ignore this basic rule of safety. Any situation can present potential threats, putting you in danger; but you can lessen your chances by being aware and taking certain steps to prevent an attack from catching you off guard. Carry your pepper spray in your purse and have it easily accessible; clip it on the inside of your purse and practice retrieving it with ease. Don't be afraid to look around – it is your business to know what is going on around you. Don't be so fixated on what you are doing that you are unaware of how close others maybe, or that your in an isolated area. When walking down a street keep away from buildings and alleys and try to walk close to the curb. Walk in the street if necessary. This minimizes the possibility of being grabbed from a doorway or building entrance. Use store windows to see reflections of others behind you. If you are being followed, you must turn to look directly at the person so he/she knows that you acknowledge their presence. If you feel threatened, decide what is the most prudent behavior. Is there a safe place to go? Get to a lighted street with people or go to a store. Walk with confidence and do not show fear. If it turns more serious, make noise by yelling "Fire" to draw attention to your self. Screaming "Help" may not draw attention and some people may not want to get involved. Do not go down a dark hallway, alley or building. Stay focused on a well-lit populated area.

If walking down the road and someone ask for directions, stay at least 6 feet away from the vehicle. It only takes seconds to be pulled into a vehicle. A grown bear can easily squeeze through a car window. Image how quickly you could be pulled through one. The best advice is ignore them and keep on walking.

In a restaurant, position yourself to face the door so you see who is coming in. Take notice of where all the exits are, including windows. In an emergency you may not be able to exit through the door that you came in. This preplanning has saved lives. Take a quick glance when you arrive in a building and familiarize yourself with the exits.

If drinking alcohol, limit your intake. A drunken woman is an easy target. Alcohol slows down your mental and physical reaction time, putting your safety at risk. To help lessen the effect that alcohol has, drink water or soda for every alcoholic beverage you consume. If you have a beer then drink a glass of water before ordering another beer. You are hydrating your system and affecting the alcohol in your blood. It is advisable to eat something along with your drink.

Mall or other outings: When shopping, avoid filling your arms with packages. Keep one arm and hand free so you can respond in a defensive manner if necessary. Never be so engaged in what you are doing that you don't know what is going on around you. Be wary of a stranger that is offering you a modeling job or other "on the spot" position. These cons approach women, teenagers and young girls and boys at malls and other shopping stores luring them outside for trial shots, then kidnapping or conning them to another location where he assaults them.

Be wary of anyone, male or female, who seems overly friendly towards you as you're leaving a building or mall. They most likely are casing you and when you leave the building you may find yourself being robbed by that friendly person. Take precautions and be safe. Find a security guard and have them escort you to your vehicle. Also, avoid overly friendly people at parks, movies, pools, beaches and hotels.

Avoid the mall's hallway restrooms and use a store or restaurant restroom. If possible go with a friend. Public restrooms are notorious for perverts. Never allow your children to go to any public restroom alone. Their safety is your responsibility and you do not know who is in there. If other adults in the bathroom are uncomfortable with your safety measures let them talk about you, and ignore the comments. Keeping your child safe is the most important job you have. Take precautions and be safe. When my children were younger I always escorted them into the ladies restroom. On occasion, women would comment on how boys should not be in the ladies restroom. I ignored the snooty remarks knowing that explaining to them would do no good, and I didn't care what they thought anyway. I was keeping my children safe and that is all that mattered to me.

I know for a fact that pedophiles will wait for a victim in a public restroom for as long as it takes.

I was in a store one day with my 5-year-old son when the entire store was put in lock down. A young boy, the same age as my son, was killed in the men's bathroom. One by one the police took our information and let us leave. The following day the newspaper reported that a pedophile waited in this local store's restroom for a young boy to come in. The pedophile sexually assaulted and strangled the child leaving the mother to find her son dead lying next to a toilet. The pedophile was caught because of the stores cameras and the help of the public. That horrible incident never left my mind. I encourage every parent to escort their child to the restroom. Never leave your child unattended. Many stores have family restrooms, so use them, because you do not know who is lurking in public restrooms.

Purse snatching: This is a crime of opportunity. Take away the opportunity from the thief. Zip your purse and keep your hand on it. When traveling or shopping do not carry your wallet in your purse, conceal it in a coat, sweater, pocket, or a fanny pack. Don't wrap the strap around your shoulder, neck or wrist. Grabbing and shoving that may take place can result in injury. Carry your purse or packages on the side away from the road. Purse snatching is committed by criminals on motorcycles and bicycles so keep your purse under your arm and be sure all compartments are closed.

Never let your purse lay open or unattended in a shopping cart, store counter or a public table. I cannot believe how many women leave their purses unattended while shopping. Keep your purse on your body. It is a quick action to steal your purse or wallet if you leave it unattended. Report a lost or stolen purse or wallet immediately to the police and The Social Security Administration line 800-269-0271. That will help if someone tries to use your cards. Never carry your Social Security card with you. Keep it in a locked safe. Only carry cash or the one credit card you will use for that shopping trip.

Don't carry all your cards with you; it's not worth the risk. Have copies of the front and back of all your cards, and keep them in a locked safe.

ATM Safety: Be aware of the surrounding area, and if you sense something wrong, do not use the machine. Go to another ATM location. When using a drive-up, keep the passenger window closed and doors locked. While at the ATM use your hand or body to protect the keypad. You do not know who may be watching or from what distance. Never leave your ATM receipt at the machine. Take it with you and shred it. Criminals have used binoculars to get your PIN number so take precautions. You can use a credit card as a weapon. Hold your card firmly between your thumb and finger, slice quickly and firmly across the assailants face. It cuts like a razor blade.

Carrying keys in a defensive manner is a good safety measure. Carry your keys the way you normally do to open your vehicle's door. Use your keys in a self-defense manner gauging the eyes or neck. You can also scrape the attackers face with the tip of your key. Do not spread them between your fingers; if you strike in that manner you will tear your own hand tissue causing extreme pain and inability to defend yourself to your best ability!

Outdoor safety: Never go hiking or camping alone. If you are that adventurous and do go alone, take as many precautions as possible to stay safe. Let other people know your location and when you plan to be back. Carry a cell phone, pepper spray and /or another weapon with you at all times. Don't rely solely on pepper spray for your safety. No woman should go to a park, a lake, a river, etc. alone. These are extremely unsafe locations.

GIRLS NIGHT OUT

Having fun and "cutting loose" is something we all enjoy. Consider taking a few safety measures to insure your time out will be a safe one.

When out on the town, use common sense and don't lower your guard. Keep your senses heightened and be aware. Listen to your instincts. "If it does not feel right, it's not right." If your instincts are telling you this guy or place is just not right, go somewhere that is well lit and where there are plenty of people. When you are out you should feel comfortable with your surroundings.

Many of my students have shared how they wish they would have listened to that little voice warning them of danger. Sadly, they did not listen to their instincts. Many have said it was because they did not want to seem immature, rude or scared. Whatever the reason, they still became a victim of crime.

If going out to a familiar or an unfamiliar area, go with a friend or friends. There is safety in numbers.

Being aware of your appearance when going out alone is important. Continue reading before you get upset with me; this is very important to understand. Women have the right to wear what they want, but if going out alone, think about your appearance. Not everyone interprets the way you dress the same way you do. Dressing in a revealing way or an expensive way, and going out alone, calls for precaution on your part. Wear a long coat; keep your expensive jewelry hidden until you arrive safely at your location. You do not want to draw attention to yourself or draw the wrong type of person to you. You do not want to attract trouble. A woman alone is an easy target for criminals.

Dressing in a loose manner, especially if alone, may be taken by a criminal that you have no respect for yourself, so why should the criminal. The sexual attacker may think you are not worthy of respect. It may sound harsh, but how you dress and act is how others portray you. Dress the way you wish, just take precautions at appropriate times. Women have the right to be independent and free, but you have to be smart about the environment your in. Don't put caution aside because that is when you are most vulnerable to danger. A woman dressed in a crisp business suit carrying herself with confidence projects to others that she has it together. A woman dressed in a revealing, low cut, tight fitting dress may be looked at as a woman with no confidence. In reality, neither may be the case, but that is what she is projecting to others. It is a sad fact in our society, and it is human conditioning, to judge others visually at first. Please do not take this out of context. I believe you can dress the way that makes you comfortable, but unfortunately, society makes it's own rules which some either choose to follow or go against. Understand, I am talking about sexual predators, not the whole society.

When out on the town be cautious at closing times of bars and nightclubs. People that had too much to drink can become obnoxious. They may be looking for trouble and may be sexual predators. Keep your pepper spray in your hand and ready to use.

An article that was in our local paper sadly reminds us that no matter how close we are to home its still not safe for a woman to walk alone. This article told about a young high school girl who only lived a few blocks from the movie theaters and was on her way home after a show. Three males pulled up, dragged her into the car, and assaulted her a few blocks away, dropping her off near the location where they snatched her off the road.

Sadly in our society, women and girls that walk alone in the daylight or evening hours are at a high risk for assault. This falls under "crime of opportunity." For your safety, wait in a well-lit, populated area for your ride, or walk with others. When walking home from school, shops, theaters or work, take precautions. It is better to wait for a safe way home than to never get home. Whenever you're out walking, be observant and stroll with energy and confidence. Remember, not everyone is looking out for your best interest.

Dating: When going out on a date, take extra precautions. I am shocked at all of the girls that have taken my course and share their bad dating experiences. Many have experienced date rape and others had to fight and run to safety.

Women should insist on meeting at public places and driving themselves for the first few dates. Double dating is always a good idea. That means staying together at one location, not one couple going one way the other couple another direction. I am referring to your first few dates; give yourself time to get to know this person better in a safe environment. I mention this during my training program attended by high school and college age females. The students will respond by mentioning how they double date but they don't stick together. They go separate ways, and many of these girls regret being left alone. So when you double date, stay together. Never leave a friend alone. One student shared her experience about double dating. She thought she took measures to be safe on her first date with a guy by asking her closest friends to double date with them. They were just hanging out at their house; the parents went out for dinner, but were returning soon. Her friends, wanting time alone before her parents came back, went to another part of the house, leaving her alone with her new date. He took advantage of that. He sexually assaulted her in the front room. She was in such shock and disbelief at what happened that she didn't say anything to her friends all night. She kept silent about this experience until she took my course. After one of the classes, she asked to speak to me in private, where she opened up. It was obvious that she felt guilty and ashamed. She expressed to me that she felt if she didn't talk about what happened to her that night, that it might not have really happened, or that all of these feelings would just go away. She did not want to acknowledge the assault, so she pushed it deep down and never recognized that she was victimized. She felt betrayed by her friends. Blaming her friends made her feel more guilty than what this young man had done to her. She had not been on a date since that evening. She also put a distance between those two friends. I listened carefully to her and shared some comforting words and advised her to talk to a counselor to start the healing process. I'm happy to state that she did take the advice, is doing well, and has a new boyfriend. Don't let this happen to your friends. Stay together on those first few dates. Be a safety net for each other.

When going out on a date let someone know your plans, like who and where you are meeting. Carry a cell phone and, if possible, check in with someone or have them call you at a designated time during your date. You can also use this as an excuse to get out of a date that is not going well.

Drive yourself for your first few dates; this is important. This may sound strange because you want your date to pick you up. But for your safety, drive or take a cab for the first few dates until you get to know this person better. Take extra precautions for your own safety. Many of the women I have taught have shared how they got themselves into an unsafe situation because they did not have their own transportation. One of my students shared this situation. On the second date, he picked her up at her home. They had reservations at a local restaurant, but he changed their dinner plans at the last minute, deciding to go to a friend's party in another town (without her consent). She did ask to be brought back home, but he convinced her it would be fun. At the party she instantly felt unsafe. Her date and his friends where trying to get her drunk. She was not into drinking alcohol or partying. She sensed something was very wrong. She knew nobody there and felt alone and scared. She called her Dad from her cell phone from the bathroom but she had no idea where she was. Her dad told her to use the home phone to dial 911 and place the receiver in an inconspicuous place so nobody would hang it up. After a while the police did arrive they found date rape drugs on the young men and alcohol in the home. One of the officers called her dad giving him directions to her location. Her dad came and safely got her. She said she felt bad for getting them in trouble, but I told this young lady that she did the right thing; she listened and trusted her gut instincts. If she would have ignored her instincts, as many young women do, and been polite and played along, she most likely would have been hurt. She shared this openly with the class that day, which started a domino effect in stories. Women can learn from other women if they just listen. Another student shared her unexpected experience after she and her date finished dinner and were going out to the parking lot. As they were walking to his car they kissed a few times. When they got inside of the vehicle he became forceful and aggressive. She shoved him off but he became even more aggressive and violent. She escaped from the vehicle and tried to get back to the restaurant but he blocked her path. He was trying to convince her to get back into his car. But the more she refused the more agitated he became. She tried calming him down by talking calmly and agreeing with him. She even tried to convince him to allow her to go back into the restaurant to use the restroom, but nothing worked. Suddenly, a thought came to her...something she recently saw on TV. She started freaking out, waving her hands and talking loudly. She started to draw attention from other people and her date got in his car and left, leaving her at the restaurant. Yes, she felt embarrassed, but she got home safely. I told her she did a great job and how imaginative she was. She kept her composure and did what she had to do to get out of a bad situation. This type of situation is another reason why you should never feel embarrassed to do what you have too to get out of an unsafe situation. You should have your own transportation or money for a cab so you can leave when you want to. You want to be able to control your safety, especially when meeting someone new; you just never know what his intentions are.

When dating someone new, ask your female friends about him. It's better to get an idea before you invest your time and safety on someone. When you ask others about his personality, values, and character, take the information with a grain of salt. Be sure to ask questions that are important to you. Ask direct questions and ask why they feel that way or what gave them that idea about that person.

After a few dates with your new boyfriend, communicate up front what your sexual limits are. State your limits clearly and ask him to repeat them back to you. That way you both will be clear.

Many rapists will try to get you to drive back with him to his place, giving the excuse that he forgot his wallet, needs to feed his pet, or needs to let the dog out, or some other excuse to get you alone in his home; and he is now in charge. For your safety, meet him at the restaurant or another location. If he insists that you go with him, pay close attention to the signs that were discussed in the "What is rape" chapter.

These signs are telling you that he is trying to control you and the situation, which is not a safe position for you to be in.

On your first few dates pay your own way or pay for a portion of the date. That way you won't "owe" him something if he spent money on you.

During your date, if you have any suspicious or weird feelings, get out of there and stay somewhere safe. Listen to your gut. If it doesn't feel right, it's not right. Intuition is never wrong!

These are things women can do to reduce their chances of assault when alone or on a date:

1   Provide your own transportation.

2   Have pepper spray with you.

3   Have the attitude and mind-set that you will protect yourself physically if you need to.

4   Carry a cell phone.

5   If it doesn't feel right, it's not right. Listen to your gut.

6   Don't drink or party to the point that you are not in control of your senses. Alcohol and drugs do slow down your reaction time and cloud your judgment, putting yourself at risk.

7   Be your own person and keep your senses about you. Do not allow someone else to control you, or convince you to do something you are uncomfortable doing. You are responsible for yourself. Don't give that power to someone else.

8   Never leave a party, bar, or anywhere with a man that you just met or you don't know very well.

9   Never accept rides from a stranger or someone you just met.

10 If you are being harassed at a bar or restaurant and you get the situation under control, do not think that it is over. Chances are that you may have offended the person's ego, and he may retaliate after you leave the bar or restaurant. Do not completely relax nor let your guard down, because danger may still be present and he may be waiting for you to leave. He may be waiting for you in the parking lot. Under these circumstances, never go to your car alone; have someone escort you for your safety. Be sure that this person is not following you.

I had two students share their story regarding this type of situation. These two friends who are co-workers went out for drinks after work one evening. A man at the bar kept buying them drinks. They kept refusing to accept the drinks. They even went as far as to ask for help from the waitress to inter-vene and not to bring them any drinks he ordered. The drinks stopped coming; the two friends thought it was over and were under the impression that the situation was resolved. In truth, the man was of-fended and he wanted to get even. The two friends left to go home, unaware that the man from the bar was following them. The guy followed them back to their office parking lot where he approached them in an aggressive manner and he began yelling threats at them. The friend who got out of the car to go to her own car, immediately got back into her friend's car, and they drove to a near by gas station, where they went inside to call their husbands. By this time the guy from the bar drove off and they never saw him again. These two ladies were lucky because it could have gotten very serious. Take extra precautions in these situations. You never know the mental stability or intentions of someone else.

Alcohol and drugs distorts reality, slows your reaction time and clouds your judgment. If something occurs, your perception about the event may become blurred and confused. Your ability to defend yourself verbally and physically declines. Alcohol enters the bloodstream within minutes, it reaches the brain and begins to affect you mentally and physically. It takes at least one hour to eliminate one drink. A 12oz beer, a mixed drink with one shot of liquor and a 5 oz glass of wine all contain the same amount of alcohol. Consider your size, weight, and food consumption and how quickly you're drinking. One of the first things affected by alcohol is the ability to use good judgment. The more alcohol you consume the more vulnerable you will seem making you more acceptable to crime. Women who are obviously drunk or high on drugs are targets to men and groups of men looking for an easy target. Don't drink to the point of not being able to control yourself or a situation. Make it your own rule to have one or two drinks then switch to water or soda. A man who is planning to take advantage of a woman will continue giving her alcohol. Don't allow anyone to keep giving you drinks. Do not make it easy for criminals; keep your wits about you. Never accept an open drink from anyone because it might have a date rape drug in it. Never leave your drink out of your sight; place your hand on top of your glass and make that a habit. They make small bottle openers that hook onto a key chain. That way you can open your own bottle and know your drink is safe.

Never, under any circumstances, leave an intoxicated friend alone or allow them to leave with someone they just met recently or that night. Many women have been attacked and/or killed by this would-be new friend. Your friend who has had too much to drink is unable to make a responsible decision. It is up to you and others to step in and keep them safe. Be a true friend intervene, do not allow them to leave with someone they just met or don't really know well. Be their logic for them because you may just save them from harm.

Never let yourself be set up. Another student's story brings this home. This young college student was raised in a very strict religious home. She was very naïve and trusted everyone. Unfortunately, the rest of the world was not looking out for her safety. Following is her experience at her first college party. She was invited to a Freshman's only party a few weeks after the new school year started. Sadly, her fellow classmates took advantage of her naiveté and kept giving her fruit flavored alcoholic drinks. She became drunk quickly. Her two new male classmates brought her in a back room and assaulted her. A female friend looking for her found her in the back room. It was apparent to her friend what had happened. She got others to help bring her back to her dorm room. Nobody called the college security or the police to report the situation, because of the alcohol. The following week this young lady did tell her parents what happened, and they took her out of school and did not report it to the police either. She started taking on-line college courses. During my last class with her, she cried often. When I asked her why, she replied that she "didn't want the classes to stop because she felt strong when she was here." That is when she shared her experience with me.

It's a hard fact of life, but you never really know who your friends are!

Date Rape Drugs can be easily slipped into your drink without you noticing. For your safety, keep your drink in sight at all times. Simply keep your hand over your glass in a relaxed manner. If you go to the dance floor, the restroom, or to visit someone at another table keep it with you or buy a new drink when you return to your table. A good strategy is to make sure you have time to finish most of your drink before you leave the table. Then you won't feel like you will offend your companions when you come back by ordering a new drink. Most of these drugs do not change the color or taste of the drink, and are odorless. There has been an increase in reports of date rape drugs being used to commit sexual assault. Take measures to ensure your safety.

The following information on date rape drugs comes from www.nida.nih.gov

Ecstasy (MDMA) is a hallucinogenic stimulant similar to speed. It comes in varies sizes, colors and shapes. They are roughly the size of an aspirin. Ecstasy comes in pill and capsule form that can be laced with other dangerous drugs such as methamphetamine and PCP, increasing the danger with ecstasy. This drug shows up at college and high school parties, bars and nightclubs. They are easily purchased at all-night dance parties. Ecstasy can easily be put into a drink without you realizing it. It will not change the color or flavor of your drink. Side effects from ecstasy are: loss of your senses, sleeplessness, confusion, severe anxiety, increased heart rate, increased blood pressure, nausea, faintness, sweating and chills, blurred vision, tremors, paranoia and rapid eye movement.

Special K (Ketamine HCL) is an anesthetic. It comes in a pill, liquid or white powder. It can easily be mixed into your drink because it is clear in color and gives the appearance of water. This drug shows up at college and high school parties, bars and nightclubs. The side effects of Special K can create paralysis from the neck down for about 15 minutes. It causes hallucinations, nausea, memory loss, unconsciousness, and can cause respiratory arrest, brain hemorrhage, coma and death.

GHB (Gamma Hydroxy Butyrate) is a natural fatty acid that secretes small amounts of hormones in the body. It is a powerful nervous system depressant that has been used in sexual assault. GHB causes euphoric and sedative effects making you very tired, similar to a tranquilizer, and making it easy for someone to sexually assault you. This drug is used in combination with Ecstasy and Special K to enhance the effects of the other. It comes in powder, tablet, capsule or liquid form. The liquid form is usually clear in color and smells like coconut oil and has a strong salty taste. It is easily mixed with liquids. The powder form has a fruity flavor and is mixed with liquids. Both forms can be mixed with any type of liquid. This drug shows up at gyms, college parties, in bars and nightclubs. Some of the side effects of GHB are drowsiness, nausea, vomiting, confusion, seizures, tremors, respiratory arrest, speech and motor skill interference, and can lead to unconsciousness, coma and death.

DXM (Dextromethorphan Hydrobromide) is a synthetic morphine analog that acts as a cough suppressant. It comes in forms of liquid, gels or tablets (cough syrup and cold tablets). This drug shows up at college and high school parties, bars and nightclubs. It can easily be dropped into someone's drink. The side effects of DXM are nausea, itchy skin, a strong sensation to dissassociate yourself from others, coma and death. DXM has been laced with ecstasy or LSD.

LSD (Lysergic Acid Diethylamide) LSD is a strong hallucinogen that alters one's mood, thoughts and perceptions. It also distorts one's sense of time and identity. LSD comes in the form of crystals, tablet, capsule, liquid and blotter paper that have absorbed the drug. It is a clear or an amber color and has a bitter taste. This drug shows up at gyms, college parties, bars and nightclubs. LSD can be absorbed in any part of the skin. Breathe mints, Pez candy, Starburst candy, gelatin squares and sugar pills have been laced with LSD in the past. The side effects from LSD include high body temperature, disorientation, increased heart rate, sleeplessness, dry mouth, memory loss, hallucinations, nausea, elevated blood pressure, twitching, coma and death.

Methamphetamine is a central nervous system stimulant that comes in the form of white powder or tablets. It has a bitter taste and is soluble in water and dissolves easily in drinks. It comes in many colors...white, pink, red, tan, brown or green. The tablets are about the size of a pencil eraser. The tablets can be flavored in grape, orange or vanilla. This drug shows up at college and high school parties, bars and nightclubs The side effects range from increased heart rate, irregular heartbeat, increased blood pressure, respiratory problems, confusion, paranoia, tremors, to cardiovascular collapse, stroke and death.

Rohypnol (flunitrazepam) is a central nervous system depressant, and it comes in liquid form. It is odorless and tasteless. This drug shows up at college and high school parties, bars and nightclubs. Rohypnol can incapacitate a victim and cause amnesia preventing them from defending against sexual assault and causing them not remember the events they experienced. The side effects are decreased blood pressure, drowsiness, dizziness, confusion, amnesia and may be lethal when mixed with alcohol and other depressants.

Facilitate your own prevention with this new knowledge. Take safety precautions when you're out in a public place; never leave your drink unattended or accept pills, candy or breath mints from someone you just met...it could be laced with a drug. These drugs in combination with alcohol can be even more dangerous. The drugs I have mentioned have been reported in sexual assault cases.

You can purchase a drug test called Drink Detective at www.drinkdetective.com. The kit can detect if your drink has been spiked with a date rape drug. The kit is small enough to fit in your pocket or wallet and works within seconds.

To get more information on date rape drugs or club drugs contact The National Institute of Drug Abuse at www.nida.nih.gov/

COLLEGE CAMPUS SAFETY

Campus Safety: I have observed from the college students that attend my program how naive females are and how they lower their guard at college. They seem to share a false sense of security. First time students will face alcohol, drugs and sex pressures. They will be new to the campus grounds, and these are problems they will face on their own. First time students are very vulnerable to assault. By the time they reach college they should know what their standards are and know what they believe in, so they don't give in to the pressures of college pranks and partying. Unfortunately for some, this may be the first time away from home, so they don't really think about the consequences of their decisions. They need to know that there is power in their decisions. That power leads to safe or unsafe situations. They may feel alone, insecure and possibly have no friends there. Students may feel as though they need to have social approval to fit in, so they jeopardize their safety among new friends. In speaking with them after class, they express that they are surrounded by others their age and feel they are safe because they are all there for the same purpose, to learn and get a degree. In reality, the students are thrown together with hundreds of strangers coming from different backgrounds, beliefs and values, putting them in danger the same as anywhere else. If you are a student attending high school or college, always be true to yourself. Don't just go along with the crowd. Own yourself because only you are accountable for you. Whether you're "talked into something," or are a willing participant, you will be held accountable. Have confidence in yourself and take responsibility for your life.

Colleges have parties with the upper classmen attending who will take advantage of the new vulnerable students. College campuses are a safe haven for sexual predators because of the naïve thoughts that students have, including unsupervised parties, ease of acquiring alcohol and drugs, and easy access to the dorms through unlocked windows and doors leading into dorm rooms. Doors are sometimes left propped open by students, or the access scan is faulty and access to unsecured buildings is made easy. You should notify campus security immediately to have these doors and locks fixed.

For your safety, never study alone in a building in the daytime or nighttime. When walking at night, stay in well-lit areas. Never take shortcuts through wooded areas or places that are not easily seen by others. Never be embarrassed to use the Campus Escort Service. Your safety comes first. Be familiar with the location of emergency call boxes and know how they work. Never put personal information on your belongings, like your key chain, bike, or books. Never give out personal information. If someone says they are verifying your information, tell them the main office has that information and they should check with them. You should contact the main office if this occurs. At one of the local campuses I taught at, someone was posing as office personnel and getting student's personal information and opening credit cards in their names. So be smart and keep your identity safe. Carry only the amount of cash you need, or one credit card. Have pepper spray on you always. Use caution in the parking lots. Keep your doors locked and windows up. Park under lights and in populated areas. Avoid parking near dumpsters and shrubs. Keep your laptop, purse, CD players and any expensive item in the back seat and covered with a towel or jacket. It is very easy to break a car window and walk off with these items.

If living on campus, keep your dorm room doors and windows locked at all times even if you are going to be gone for a short time. Never leave notes on your door that you are not in and where you can be found. This is telling others your room is vacant. Go with your friends to the laundry and shower room. Stay observant and be careful. Keep a flash light and pepper spray with you at these locations. I have had many college students tell me that while they were in the shower and laundry areas someone turned off the lights and tried to harm them. In all of the situations they screamed immediately, drawing attention to themselves. Be cautious at your campus because not everyone is looking out for your safety. Keep the residence halls doors locked and don't prop the doors open so others can easily enter. This puts you and everyone else at risk of a crime. Be sure all your roommates follow the same safety precautions. Use a door alarm for added safety in your dorm room.* If attending fraternity parties, never go in a back room or the upstairs bedrooms because these are isolated rooms were many sexual attacks do occur. Find out if the college you attend offers rape awareness programs and get a report from the administrators on campus crimes. Report all criminal acts to the Campus Police. Follow the suggestions in the dating section while attending parties.

(* to purchase a door stop alarm go to www.getcourage.com)

DOMESTIC VIOLENCE

Domestic Violence is a problem that cuts across age, income and social status. Domestic violence constitutes any type of verbal, physical or sexual abuse. The techniques in this book will help you defend yourself and hopefully empower you with self-worth, confidence and the strength to get out of a violent relationship. A violent relationship is highly unlikely to change for the better. Studies show that domestic violence gets worse. If domestic violence has happened once, chances are it is likely to occur again. Many domestic violence attacks occur because of alcohol, money problems, unemployement, jealousy, a desire to 'put you in your place', wanting power and control in the relationship, and some form of humiliation. The victim of domestic violence is programmed by the attacker to think she is to blame for this violent act...that she triggered this action herself and deserves the pain. Never blame yourself nor let someone make you think that way. Nobody deserves to be hit, pushed, kicked, bullied or belittled. Muster up the strength and courage to get help.

One of the ladies taking my program shared her experience of domestic violence with me. She said that her husband was a caring, loving and supportive man the first two years of their marriage. She truly felt they had the perfect relationship. They decided together after their second child was born that she would be a stay at home mom. Delighted with the idea, she didn't realize that this was the birthing of her nightmare for the next five years. In less than a year's time, the finances became tight. The yelling was continuous; drinking became a nightly ritual for her husband. Verbal abuse was the beginning, then physical abuse soon followed. The first beating was in a fit of drunken rage; at least that is what she wanted to believe. The beatings started out a few times a month, then progressed to weekly. She truly believed he was sorry each and every time, and that that would be the last time. She convinced herself of that reasoning for five years. During this time she said she was so humiliated that she no longer visited her friends or relatives. When they were invited somewhere, she made up stories about the kids being sick or that they had other commitments. She lived in solitude and abuse for five years. She mentioned how every once in a while she mustered up the strength to leave, but then she realized how scared she was of him. She also felt that she needed him to live. She truly believed he loved her.

For five long, painful years she lived in this dark, dismal life. The last beating she took was worse than all the other times. During the last beating she sustained, he was verbally abusing her; not that that was unusual, but his voice was more bitter and hateful than the other times. As he repeatedly kicked her in the stomach, something in her snapped and she knew deep down she had to leave, or the next time she would be killed. That night for the first time she found the courage to leave him physically and mentally. As he lay passed out later that evening, she reported him to the police and had him arrested. She moved in with her parents and began to rebuild her life. I met her three years later at one of my self-defense classes. She is living safely with her kids in a happy, stable home that she owns.

To look at her, one would think that she was always a confident, strong willed woman, and that she would never be in an abusive relationship. Domestic violence can occur to any woman with no regard to status in society, occupation, or confidence. What is important is that you realize it is wrong and dangerous, and that you can change your circumstances. It takes courage to accept it and take the steps to get help.

What moved me personally was how she had the inner strength to share her nightmare of five years with someone she hardly knew. I believe she shared her story with me because it empowered her; it gave inner strength and ownership of what she went through, which gave her more positive power in herself. It is a cleansing effect that I think most people need so they can move on, leaving the bad experience behind them and looking to the future. One question I asked her was, "Why did you not ask for help from your family or friends early on?" Her response was that she felt she could fix it on her own. She was too proud to admit that she was allowing this to happen to her. She said looking back on the situation that she continuously convinced herself that he really didn't mean to hurt her and things would get better. She admitted that she knew this was no way to live, but didn't want to face the truth that she was becoming a victim of domestic violence, so she chose to stay in an abusive relationship until something snapped inside her...the fear of death. That fear of death became reality the last night she was beaten. That was what woke her up and gave her the strength to make a change for herself and her two children. She shared how she looks back now and realizes how she and her kids lost five years of life. She wishes she would have had the courage and strength to have left him the first time the abuse occurred. She repeatedly mentioned how sorry she was for being too proud, and for thinking he truly loved her. She realizes now that he never unequivocally loved her. She finished by saying, "If someone loves you they would never beat you or dehumanize you".

I have never experienced domestic violence ....she opened my eyes. Women that are in this situation feel as though they are stuck and have no way out. Their pride in themselves confuses them into thinking they can make this better or fix this situation, when in reality no one can fix this type of abuse alone. For these women, domestic violence starts to rule their life instead of them ruling their own life. It also seems that they want so badly to believe that this abuse will magically disappear. If she has dinner on the table, if she can keep the kids a bit more quiet, if he gets a raise,... That is why they continue to stay in a horrific relationship year after year that others not living in it can't understand. I believe they see their life as a dream of what can be. Blinding themselves of the reality of what there life truly is. It is a roller coaster way of life for these women. I've always asked myself, "How can a woman live that way? Why live that way? Just leave the SOB." Now I have a better understanding of how women get trapped and sucked into this way of living. Months, sometimes years go by before they really understand for themselves that this is not their fault and the situation is never going to end nor get better, and that it only gets worse.

If you are in a violent relationship, please read and reread this chapter and muster up the courage and follow these suggestions. No person should tolerate a demeaning behavior or be dehumanized by anyone.

If living in a violent relationship and children are involved, you can't leave them. So do what you must to protect yourself and your loved ones from harm. Call the police immediately. Have a child go to a neighbors and call for help. If violence does occur, use the techniques taught in this book to protect yourself. You have to mentally and physically be strong. You may feel as though you love this person and hold back – that is the worse way to think because it will weaken your abilities. One of the hardest feelings to get over and accept is the feeling of betrayal by someone you thought loved and cared for you.

If you fight back, fight to win. You must be vicious, because his intent was to humiliate you and cause you bodily harm. Nobody deserves that. You are a valuable person, so believe in yourself and your abilities. Once the situation is over and / or the police have arrived, you must decide what you are going to do. This will be a life changing decision for you. You must decide if you can work this out or if it has become a regular pattern. If both parties, agree to counseling, that is a step in the right direction. If you know, deep down you know, that things will never change, then get aid through local domestic violence agencies. Shelter or legal aid is available. The police can put you in touch with the right agencies. Take the legal steps necessary to get out of an unhealthy, dangerous relationship. Do not feel that you are alone. There are wonderful, trusting people and agencies that will help you and your children.

Following are warning signs to look out for and to take seriously.

1. Refusing to hear "NO" is a clear sign of trouble in any context.

2. Belittles you either in front of friends or when alone.

3. Controls your personal environment, your hairstyle, hair color, your clothes, friends, how you should dress, etc.

4. Controls who you socialize with.

5. Will state that you are a "tease in front of other men" by the way you move, the clothes you wear, they way you talk, …

6. Gets jealous.

7. Ease drops on your phone calls / monitors your calls.

8. Always chooses where to eat, what movie to see, activities to do, plans everything.

9. Wants to know where you are at all times.

10. Checks your car's odometer reading.

11. Physically grabs or pushes you.

12. Intimidates you.

13. Uses his body to block your path.

14. Easily hot tempered.

15. Doesn't treat you as an equal.

16. Enjoys bulling you, others or animals.

17. Drinks and / or does drugs; wants you to join him or he belittles you if you don't.

18. Is rude and belittling to other women for no reason.

Never allow your husband or boyfriend to hurt you or make you feel belittled. Be bold and courageous. Have faith in yourself. Abuse thrives on secrecy. If you or someone you know is in an abusive relationship help yourself and / or them to get out of it safely.

Abuse hotline: 800-656-4673 or 800-799-7233.

For more information on Domestic Violence go to www.nsvrc.org or call 800-799-SAFE

PUBLIC TRANSPORTATION

Taxis: It is safe to use taxis when going out alone or meeting someone. You will be dropped off and picked up at a safe location. A safe location would be in front of the theater, restaurant, or a well-lit, busy shop. When using a taxi, keep the taxi company information with you. When the taxi arrives be sure it is the correct taxi company. When returning home, have your door key ready and ask the driver to wait until you get inside before leaving. Be careful of public transportation because there are pirate cab drivers (gypsy taxi's) all over the world; be alert and listen to your instincts. Be aware of unmarked cabs and only take cabs that are officially marked. Many restaurants or nightclubs offer a cab service and know of a reliable taxi company. As a safety precaution, book your taxi in advance from a reputable cab company. You can ask for the name and number of your driver. Never enter a taxi if it is not the one you booked in advanced. Use common sense.

If you cannot book your taxi in advance when leaving a restaurant, ask the manager to call for a taxi. Most restaurants use a local company. Again, ask for the cab name. You can even ask for the registered cab number. If hailing a cab from the street, get a taxi from a cabstand rather than hailing one coming down the street. Pirate taxis, which have unlicensed drivers, wait until the registered cabs are gone, then pick up passengers. Be sure to ask your driver questions before entering the cab.

Buses, Subways, and Trains: While traveling on any public transportation you need to stay alert for pick-pocketers, muggers and sexual predators. Try to be in the view of the driver or sit closest to the driver and the door. Sit with other passengers and avoid being isolated. There is safety in numbers. Keep your belongings close to you; do not put them on an empty seat near you, which is very easy for a snatch-n-grab as someone leaves the bus or train. Secure your belongings between your legs on the floor or place them on your lap. Be familiar with the routes and times of arrival. Have back up routes in case of an emergency. Don't nap; stay alert and aware of what is going on around you. It is not wise to make small talk with strangers on your trip. This could become too friendly and become suggestive, which puts you in a dangerous situation. Be wary of overly friendly people; you may find yourself being robbed by that friendly person when you get to your departure point. If someone is making you uncomfortable, move. Be assertive vocally and have pepper spray ready. On some trains there are guards, so be sure to get their attention and calmly explain your complaint. Think your way out of the problem confidently.

Airport safety: Common sense goes a long way and it applies here. Never accept anything from someone at the airport. Never leave your luggage, purse, brief case, or laptop out of your sight. Keep your belongings between your legs while standing in line or sitting. Don't walk around holding your ticket. I have seen people drop their ticket without realizing it. Keep your ticket and ID in a secure compartment and keep it closed. Keep all medicines, expensive jewelry and other valuable items in your carry-on and never let it out of your sight. A good idea is to have average looking luggage. Criminals are looking for the expensive stuff to steal. Airport parking lots are easy to get lost in. There are different levels and sections, all marked in letters, colors and numbers, so be sure to write down your exact parking space. If lost, never show it, because fear is like radar to criminals. Stay calm and go back to the main airport. Locate the airport security office and have them help you locate your vehicle. Never be embarrassed to use the security services. They are happy to help.

DRIVING SAFETY

What is the very first thing you should do when you get in your car? LOCK your doors. Lock your doors before you put the key in the ignition or secure seatbelts. After you have locked your doors start your ignition, put the vehicle in gear and then put your seatbelt on. There have been women kidnapped out of their locked vehicles by an assailant using his voice as a weapon. He commands her to "open the door". The assailant did not display a weapon. He had a commanding voice and unfortunately she listened to his command. If she had the vehicle in gear she could have left immediately. That is why you lock your doors start the ignition, put the vehicle in gear and then secure your seatbelt. It only takes a few seconds. Crime only takes a few seconds. Think about it. You just left the mall you get in your vehicle and within seconds someone is banging on your window commanding you to open the door! He is not pointing a weapon at you. What are you going to do? Freeze up and listen to this criminal, or stay calm and leave immediately because you already have your vehicle in gear. The next time you're out, put yourself in that situation. Practice the steps above and make them a habit every time you get in your vehicle.

AAA service and a cell phone are excellent choices to make your travels safer. You can use your cell phone for an emergency and AAA services offer towing, gas delivery, and other worthwhile services. Check your local area for road services.

Have an **emergency kit** in your vehicle. (first aid kit, water, blanket, warm clothes, a flashlight, boots, ice melt, metal shovel, non-perishable snacks, call police sign, pepper spray, reflectors or flares, medication you need regularly, auto fire extinguisher) Check your emergency kit periodically and update for the season.

The key to safe driving is to expect the unexpected; be a good **defensive driver**. Driver's need to exercise good judgment. Look as far down the road as possible for other vehicles, animals or debris in the road. Keep your eyes on the break lights of the vehicle in front of you as well as the vehicles in front of them; that way you will have more time to respond to a situation. Check your mirrors often. Always know what is near you and behind you, and never tailgate. When approaching an intersection, it is your responsibility to observe all the directions to oncoming traffic even if you do have the right-of-way. Every driver needs to be observant of those around them. Stay alert and be a good defensive driver.

When **driving in fog** turn on the low lights, not the high beams. Use your defroster and windshield wipers. Drive at a slower speed but reduce your speed gradually. Don't ride your brakes or slam on the brakes. Don't tailgate, have three skip markers between you and the vehicle in front of you. Don't make any sudden moves; keep your distance. Don't drive, if possible, or wait at a local restaurant or shop until visibility is better.

Plan before you go on a trip. Make sure your car is in good working condition. Whenever possible, let someone know your routes. That way if something happens they know where to look first. If your **car breaks down**, do not get out unless you are knowledgeable about vehicles. Getting out of your vehicle could cause you to be hit by an on coming vehicle or truck. Only get out of your vehicle if your life is in danger. Otherwise stay in your vehicle and keep your seat belt on. Pull as far off the road as possible for your safety as well as emergency personnel. Use your emergency flashers and put out a "call police" sign. Make note of your surroundings, street signs, mile markers and buildings. This will help them locate you faster. Call AAA, your mechanic or a friend to assist you. Do not put the vehicle's hood up because it blocks your vision from anyone stopping in front of you and walking up on your vehicle. Keep doors locked and windows up. If it is warm outside, unroll your windows about an inch and no further. You do not want someone to be able to reach their arm through the window. It is better to be sweating in the sun than be hurt. If someone stops to offer assistance, politely say that you just called the police and they are on their way. Again, never get out of your vehicle even if he states he is a mechanic. I had a student who had her car break down on the highway and a man stopped and told her he was a mechanic, and if she would get out of the car and open the hood he would fix the car for her. Without hesitation she got out of the car and opened the hood. He immediately smacked her in the face, dragged her to the side of her vehicle and assaulted her. She dragged herself into her car and called the police. He was never found. Wait for the proper help even if that means sitting in a hot car. If someone does offer help and he will not take no for an answer, call the police and stay on the line with them. Give the operator as much detailed information of the person and his vehicle as possible. Tell the persistent person that you are talking to the police and they are on their way. Stay in your vehicle until the police have arrived. Stay as calm as possible.

If you have no other choice but to leave your disabled vehicle to walk to get help, stay on the busy roads. Don't take short cuts or accept a ride from a stranger. Carry your pepper spray in the ready position. Do not leave information about where you're headed on your inside window. You never know who may come upon your vehicle to investigate it and possibly to try to follow you and cause you harm. If your disabled vehicle will not be able to be towed for 48 hours, notify the local police where the vehicle was left and advise them of the situation and when it will be moved. The State Police may have your vehicle towed elsewhere without your knowledge.

Road rage is unfortunately happening more and more. People are less patient and seem to be in a rush causing stress levels to be high. If you encounter an aggressive driver don't make eye contact or challenge the driver. Attempt to get out of the way and stay safe. Don't cut other drivers off because this can cause **road rage.** Be a courteous driver and keep your cool when traveling on the roads. Driving is a privilege and we should give it our full attention every time we get behind the wheel. We are responsible not only for ourselves but also for those around us. Stay alert and be a good defensive driver.

While driving around town be careful not to tailgate. This action can get you pinned between two cars (a common **car jacking** technique). One car will be stopped in front of you and another car will close in tightly behind you. If you did not leave yourself enough space to move around the first vehicle, you could be pinned in and car jacked or robbed. Always leave yourself an out. When stopping, stay far enough away from the vehicle in front of you so you can pull out quickly from the vehicle in case something does occur. It also helps if you get hit from the back because you will have less chance of hitting the vehicle in front of you.

If you notice a paper or item on your back windshield as you get into your vehicle do not get out of your vehicle to remove it. Leave and go to a busy, populated well-lit area. Car-jackers use this ploy to get you out of your running vehicle and they jump in, speeding off with your personal items and your keys not only to your vehicle, but to your home as well. Another ploy is to have an animal lay near or behind your vehicle to get you to assist in care of the animal. The attacker will then assault you or kidnap you. Be cautious when anyone is near your vehicle. Here is another ploy...an assailant will approach your vehicle stating that you dropped money. He will want you to open your door or roll down the window. Remember criminals may appear nice and polite but they are conning you to get what they want. That is control over you.

Don't leave your vehicle running unattended to use the ATM or to run into the gas station or quick mart. It could be easily stolen, and if you left children in the vehicle they are now in great danger. Take a few minutes to get them out of their car seat and bring them in with you. Never leave your child in a vehicle. It is unsafe under any circumstance. Don't put your convenience over the safety of your child. You don't want to regret it later.

Don't leave your wallet, purse, laptop, electronic devices etc. on the front seat. This is tempting to criminals and it is easy to break your side window and steal your personal belongings. Place your personal items in the back seat or on the floor covered with a towel or jacket. It is a good idea for women to place a man's tie or jacket in the vehicle. It gives the impression that you are not traveling alone. When traveling by vehicle and you hang your skirts and dresses from the vehicles hook, place your clothes in a travel bag, or place a man's jacket between the window and your clothes. This will give the impression that you are not traveling alone, and works as a deterrent. You can purchase an inexpensive man's jacket or tie at a consignment shop or Goodwill.

Scan your car before entering and always check the back seat. Make it a habit. As soon as you get into your car, lock the doors and leave. Do not sit in your car and make a list, or write in your checkbook or work on your laptop. This is a perfect opportunity for an attacker to get in the passenger side or even the driver's side with or without a weapon, and kidnap you. Criminals often wait in parking lots to see if someone will leave their doors unlocked. Always lock your doors. When pumping gas, lock your doors and keep your keys with you. Use the pay at the pump gas stations, which are very convenient, and you never have to leave your vehicle and your kids are always in sight.

If you are in a **fender bender** and you suspect that it was on purpose, drive to the nearest well-lit populated gas station or police station and report it. Don't doubt your instincts. If it was legit the other vehicle will follow you. Tell them you felt scared and suspicious about the accident. Call the police and give them as much detailed information on the location such as where the accident occurred, the vehicle involved and persons in the vehicle. One of my students was in a fender-bender and said she immediately knew something was wrong. A vehicle gently bumped into her vehicle at a four-way stop. Three guys got out of the car. She immediately noticed that they did not stop to look at the cars for damage, which is normally what one does when in an accident. Two of the guys came up to the passenger side door. The driver came up to her door and tried to force it open. She immediately knew this was not good and that she was in danger. She sped off and went to the first convenient store to call the police. Here again, they were not caught but she escaped safely. I would say she did the right thing. Listen to your gut because it never lies.

Be aware of **driving ploys**. If driving alone or even if you have a passenger and **someone signals that something is wrong** with your car, do not stop. Drive to the nearest gas station or well-lit and populated area. One of the ploys that has been used to get women to pull over is when a vehicle pulls up beside you flagging you down, yelling, honking or pointing at your car. They shout or gesture that you are leaking gas, oil or some other fluid or your taillight is out. Never pull over. Go to a well-lit populated area to investigate it yourself. Another ploy, which usually occurs on back roads is the driver behind you will flash his high beams at you. Trying to get you to pull over. Don't. This is a dangerous ploy that has gotten many women raped. Never pull over for anyone for any reason no matter what kind of signal or sign they may be gesturing. Get to a well-lit populated area to investigate it yourself. Exercise good judgment; many women get taken advantage of while driving so remember your safety comes before anything else. Don't pull over!

Being followed is a scary situation. You never want to go home. Drive to the nearest police station, but only during regular working day hours. Many police stations do not have an officer at the station in the evening hours; they are usually on the road or at calls. The same goes for an ambulance house and fire departments. It is best to get to a well–lit, populated store, a hospital emergency room or a busy area. Stay in your car and lay on the horn. You want to draw attention to yourself. Do not get out of your vehicle until you know that it is safe. Then report it to the police. Try to give them as much information of the driver, license plate number and a description of the vehicle.

To be certain if someone is following you, make four right hand turns, and if they are still behind you, you know something is wrong. Many of the participants that attend my program have had similar experiences that they shared, especially those that were leaving a party late at night, and those that left a bar at closing time. Thankfully they did the right thing and were able to stay safe. They were aware of the danger and they never went straight home. They drove to another location where there were plenty of people around. Most of the females went to a boyfriend's house or the college security office.

Be smart. Stay alert and aware at all times. Never let your guard down.

If you are **being followed** by a vehicle with flashing **blue lights** in an unmarked car, do not pull over. Chances are that it is an imposter. It is inexpensive and simple to install a red or blue light in any vehicle. You can purchase colored lights at any electronic store. Don't take everything at face value because your safety comes first. In this situation, turn on your dome light or flashers and wave your hand to notify the officer, if legitimate, that you recognize them but that you are going to a safe well-lit populated area to pull over. At the same time call 911 and see if the officer called it in. The dispatcher will be able to tell you if the officer is legitimate because officers call in the location, vehicle make, model and occupants in the vehicle for their own safety. Take all the precautions you can. Drive the speed limit and get to a well-lit populated area. Ask the dispatcher to send out a marked police car to your location. Remain in your vehicle. If it is a legitimate officer, explain to them calmly that you were scared. Never get out of your vehicle until you are in a safe location. One of my students shared her story of being pulled over by a guy with a blue light on his truck. He was a fireman and was pissed at her because she cut him off a few miles back. He got her to pull over because we law-bidding citizens are programmed to do so. She did not give it a second thought that this was not a real police officer. He stormed out of his truck shouting at her while standing on the side of the highway. She was frozen with fear. She just sat there stunned until he left. This could have ended a lot worse for her. He had complete control of her and the situation. Be cautious and use common sense when on the roads. You do have rights, but also remember that driving is a privilege. Obey the laws and always be respectful to the police.

No permit is required to install red or blue lights on a vehicle. Most of your unmarked police and sheriff vehicles will have one or more revolving / flashing red or blue lights with an audible warning system. Ambulance personnel, volunteer firefighters, certified search and rescue SCUBA divers, coroners and some dog handlers used in tracking humans use the blue lights when en route to an emergency call. They must still comply with the law and vehicle codes. You are not required to pull over for them. It is a courtesy. I always pull out of their way. If it were my loved one that needed help I would want rescuers to get there as soon as possible.

Let's address **being forced off the road**. I had this experience while living in NC. My children were asleep in the back seat and I was headed for the airport taking back roads. I had a man in a truck pull along side me. He was yelling something out of his passenger side window I took a quick glance and realized his intentions are not good. The split second I looked away he came over into my lane, I glanced back at him and he was making sexual gestures. He sped up, cut over in front of my car nearly hitting the front bumper and slowed down. I let off the gas took a quick glance to the opposite side of the road noticing there was no vehicles coming my way. I veered around him going into the oncoming traffic lane.   He sped up again, tailgating me, flashing his bright lights, honking his horn, yelling out the window to pull over, continuously trying to pass me. I remember getting really angry at this point. My children were still asleep in the backseat, and all I could think of is "if this idiot hits my car I am going to rip his F------ head off. Not the one he uses to think with either." My motherly instincts were really kicking in now! I knew I had a few more miles to go before I could get to the quick mart, so I kept myself calm by singing "Twinkle, Twinkle Little Star" (that was my daughter's favorite song at the time) and staying focused on not allowing him to control the road. I now had the quick mart in sight and drove straight up to the door, laying on my horn. I saw the truck pass the quick mart and a few guys came running out of the store. I explained what occurred. The clerk immediately went back in and called the police. One of the other guys stayed outside with me and his friend jumped in his truck to find the guy to get the trucks license plate. Thankfully my children slept through this ordeal because it was quit a frightening experience. According to the police officer this incident was not that uncommon, especially on the back roads. The description of the man and his truck was all too familiar to him. I was not the first person who reported this situation with the same vehicle descriptions.

Here again, keep your head clear and your mind calm. Think of your loved ones and do what you have too to stay safe. Singing kept me from holding my breath and also relaxed my muscles. My children kept me sane, because their safety was in my hands.

If you see someone having car trouble do not stop. You can be helpful without risk to yourself. Use your cell phone or drive to a station and report the trouble to the police or highway patrol. Give details like location, make, model and the color of the vehicle. Don't put your safety at risk. There have been reports of ploys where someone will look like they have car trouble and flag down vehicles for help; and you, the "good Samaritan", wind up getting robbed. Don't put your safety at risk.

If you've been in an auto accident, safely move all vehicles off busy roads. Call the police. Exchange names, addresses, phone numbers, and insurance information of everyone involved. Make notes of how the accident happened while it is fresh in your mind. At some point, call your auto insurance company, and call their insurance company to be sure they reported it, to get everything processed as soon as possible. Don't rely on the other parties to report it.

Parking lots can be scary for any one, particularly for women. They are not always well lit. They have multiple levels where you're isolated from the public and there are usually no other people around. You may have to take stairways, which are isolated and not well lit. Vehicles and pillars block your view and are easy for someone to hide behind. Taking safety measures in parking lots and parking garages is important. Park your vehicle under or near lights. Make a mental note of where you parked. Write it down if you are in a large lot. That way it will be less confusing on your trip back. Make a note of any odd item or construction going on because this will let you know you are getting close to your vehicle on your return trip. Be sure to lock your windows and doors and close your sunroof.

On your trip back to your vehicle if a van is parked next to you, get in on the passenger side. Don't feel uncomfortable doing this because it could save you from being kidnapped. Many serial killers kidnap their victims by pulling them into their van while women are trying to get into their own vehicle. Be alert and listen to your intuition. As soon as you are in your vehicle, lock the doors. If you have the keypads you can lock the door even before you're in the car. Just open the door and then lock it so that the door is locked before you even have your rear on the seat. Make it a habit to close and lock the doors immediately then start your engine. Put the car in gear and then put your seat belt on.

Be aware of vehicles parked next to you as you exit and re-enter your vehicle. Do not park near trash dumpsters, shrubs and trees that hide you from being seen by traffic. Never park in an isolated area; you want to be seen by the public. Before you get to your vehicle you should scan the surrounding area looking for anything suspicious such as someone just standing around. Always have your pepper spray ready and be prepared to use it. As you are walking up to your vehicle take a quick glance under it. It is not a myth that a rapist will hide under your car. I had a co-worker in Florida who was attacked in the parking lot of an upscale restaurant after she got off work late one night. Her attacker was waiting under her car. He grabbed her ankles, forcing her head to hit the car next to hers and then hit the pavement. She was immediately knocked unconscious. He assaulted her right there on the restaurant parking lot between two cars. Her co-workers found her. We were furious when we found out that this rapist was assaulting women at the local mall and other restaurants at closing time. Nobody knew about this rapist because it was not reported in the newspaper or being reported on the news. Why? Not everything gets reported to the public. That is why it is so important to take all possible safety measures you can. After that attack, the chefs at the restaurant escorted all waitresses to their vehicles. If you work late hours and have to go to your vehicle alone, don't. Ask someone to escort you or leave in a group and be sure everyone gets in their car safely...not just to their car but safely in their car. If that is absolutely impossible, then use good judgment when going to your car alone. If it does not feel right then turn around and go back in the direction you just came from. Carry your pepper spray in the ready position and be ready to use it.

Carrying your **keys** in the ready position when approaching your vehicle is an excellent safety measure. You can easily cause serious bodily damage to an attacker by thrusting your keys into your attackers eyes or throat. You could scrape the keys across an attackers face causing the assailant to be stunned, giving you time to retreat to safety, or striking forcefully if you have no other option.

Never give all your keys to anyone, including mechanics and parking lot attendants. Give them only the ignition key. It is not complicated to make duplicate keys. Now they have your house key and your address. How would someone know your address, you ask? Simple... it is easy to access your personal information from your license plate, and you most likely have your vehicle registration and insurance information in your glove compartment, which contains personal information. Criminals are not all stupid.

Never hide a spare key in or on the outside of your car. Car thieves know all the hiding places. If you must, keep an extra one in your wallet or purse.

Vehicle car- jacking / Kidnapping: Criminals may demand their victim to get into a vehicle. DON'T! Never go to a second location because your chance of survival at the second location is slim to none; your chance of survival increases at the first location. Do what you must at the first location even if threatened with a weapon. That is why practicing your self-defense techniques are crucial. If threatened by a criminal either in your front or back seat with a gun, do not drive off. Put the car in drive, lay on the gas and floor it, wreck your vehicle so the air bags deploy. Crash into a curb, an unoccupied parked car, a stop sign, a pole… You want to make a scene! Run as fast as you can to a safe area.

   What to do if thrown into a trunk of a car: Try to avoid getting in is your first defense. Plant one foot on top the vehicle where the car and trunk meet. Plant your other foot on the bottom of the vehicle where the car and trunk meet. Try to twist into him using your hands to gouge his eyes or dig your knuckle or thumb into his hollow portion of his throat. Try to hold onto him because when you hurt him he will let you drop, so be prepared for that possibility. Yell loudly. Remember, yelling keeps you breathing. As soon as your feet hit the ground, run as fast as you can, or if you must strike him again, do so to immobilize your attacker until he can't harm you, and you can retreat to safety.

   Worse case: if you are placed in the trunk, kick out the back taillight and stick your hand or foot out and wave like crazy. The driver will not be able to see you but everyone else will. Newer model vehicles have an emergency handle to release the trunk if locked inside.

   If you're the driver or the passenger in the front seat, grab the gear shifter and force it into another gear. Do this at a slow speed. Be ready for a quick jar and run from the car to a well-lit and populated area. This has to be done quickly, and you must be mentally prepared to escape quickly and swiftly. You will have an adrenaline rush so use it to your advantage. Timing is important.

   If placed in the front, blind the kidnapper by jabbing his eyes with your fingers or another small sharp object. Do this when the vehicle is at a slow speed or stopped. Escape quickly and run to the nearest populated area. Don't hold your breath while attempting to do this; be sure to keep breathing.

   If you are in the back of the vehicle, secure a shirt or jacket over the driver's head and hold tight using your body weight against the back seat to help your grip. Hold tight until the car stops or crashes. Do this when the vehicle is at a slow speed. Run to a well-lit, populated area. Don't look back, just run and yell 'Fire, Fire". You want to draw as much attention to yourself as possible.

   If you're the driver and the kidnapper is the passenger, you can still be very effective by using your fingers or a small sharp object to push into the eye or throat of the attacker. Be sure to strike the hollow or sides of the throat. Your keys or a pen would make a very good weapon to use, and they are at your disposal. Having pepper spray located in an inconspicuous place near the drivers seat is a great idea. You can tape a unit out of sight, but within arms reach, such as near your seat adjustor. You can spray your kidnapper and escape. (NOTE: Be sure your pepper spray unit is designed for vehicles)

   If a kidnapping is taking place in a public place where there are people, do not listen to the assailant's commands. If he states "Don't scream" or " Be quite or I'll hurt you", make all the noise you can and be boisterous. His intention is too hurt you, so do not listen to his commands. If you can knock over something such as a display or items on a counter, knock over anything that is near you trying to get the attention of other people to look your direction.

   If there is nothing to knock over, drop to the ground shaking your hands and legs wildly. Never be embarrassed to draw attention to yourself.

   The goal is to draw attention to the situation so act crazy and be loud, because this can save your life! The attacker is likely to leave because of the witnesses and possible embarrassment that you caused. I had a young college student that just finished the self-defense program and went out of state to visit friends. She stopped at a rest stop and while walking to the restrooms a man approached her, closed in on her space and commanded her to come with him, using a violent overtone. She dropped to the ground and started to shake her arms and legs wildly. The guy ran off immediately. Strangers thought she was having convulsions and called the police and ambulance. She listened to what I suggested to do in that type situation. She saved her own life!

WORK PLACE SAFETY

Workplace Safety: Most people feel secure in their workplace and they naturally lower their guard. Crime can occur in and around your workplace. You should still make it a priority to stay alert and be aware of what is going on around you in your office or at your place of work. Anyone can become a victim of a workplace assault. Be relaxed, but observant. If you notice a suspicious person coming into the building, notify security. It is just as much your responsibility to be observant, as it is the security guards job. Be observant and take action to reduce the risk of violence. Keep the company security number near your phone. It is always better to be safe than sorry. Be a responsible person.

If a co-worker is acting strangely by showing signs of hostility, making threats, stating irrational ideas, showing lack of safety for others or themselves, notify your supervisor. Some work places have a hotline set up for anonymous reports, so use this hotline when the need arises, because you could save yourself and your fellow workers from harm. If your company does not offer a hotline, you could initiate one. Workplace violence is not just committed by employees or former employees. In some cases the threat came from customers, family members or complete strangers. So make it part of your job to stay alert.

There are measures you can take to avoid being a victim of crime. Make it a habit to leave together with your co-workers. If you must work late try to coordinate it with another co-worker so you will not be alone in the building. If your company has security guards, notify them that you will be working late.

If it is impossible for you to have a working buddy, be sure to have someone walk you to your vehicle or to the public transportation area. Ask security to escort you. Keep your vehicle windows, doors and the sunroof locked even if your company has private parking lots. As soon as you get in your vehicle, lock the doors.

Report to the appropriate persons any broken security lights in the parking lot, stairwells or around the building. Bright external lights on parking lots, stairwells and buildings can decrease the risk of assault.

If you do the bank deposits for your company, keep the bank bag in a briefcase or in an inconspicuous bag. Take different routes and change your time so you are not in a set schedule of going to the bank.

Be aware of people who you work with. Some people behave differently at work than when away from the office. Don't take your relationships at face value. Not everyone is looking out for your best interest. Never announce your travel plans or that you will be away from home for a period of time; not everyone that is listening may be trustworthy, and when you return back home you may find it to be empty. Wait until you get back from your trip to share what a wonderful time you had.

Be smart about trusting co-workers with your belongings. Always lock your purse and other personal items in your drawer. If you have to pay for a locksmith, pay the bill for it; you won't be sorry. Temptation may get the better of one of your co-workers, so make it easy for all and keep your valuables locked away.

For personal safety, know where all of the fire exits and fire extinguishers are located in the building and on all floors. Suggest to your company to invest in closed-circuit cameras, alarms or panic buttons for added safety and security.

Ask your company's human resources division to arrange a self-defense course for the employees.

If you are being **sexually harassed** report it immediately to your superior. Many women will try to ignore it or wait it out. There is no waiting out sexual harassment. It will only progress, making your life miserable, and work performance will suffer. This person will see this as weakness on your part, so stand up for yourself. Sexual harassment demands immediate action. Verbalize that you do not appreciate it and that this has made you feel uncomfortable. Many times men just need to be reminded that this action is unacceptable. Most men do not want to offend you.

One of my participants is a welder and she is the only female at her work. Until she took my class she listened to their dirty jokes and sexual innuendos, which made her feel belittled and frustrated. She talked to me about this situation and I suggested that she be verbal with her co-workers and tell them exactly how she feels when listening to their jokes and remarks. Her report back to me the following week was positive with the exception of one. Her fellow co-workers apologized and did not continue that behavior around her. She truly appreciated their gesture and sincerity. The hold out came around after she got him alone and expressed her feelings about how his remarks made her feel. They all have a better working relationship and stronger communication with each other.

Workplace harassment must be stopped immediately. If this occurs again after the first verbal warning, start logging all the details of each event, such as what was said, your location, the date and time, who was present or may have heard or seen you with this other person, and how often this occurred. You can use a voice recorder to record the harassment. Keeping records is to your benefit.

Stalking - If you are being stalked or have a restraining order against someone, notify and give a picture of the stalker to your boss, security guards and co-workers. It is your responsibility to others that are in your life to know of an unsafe situation. That way everyone can look out for your safety as well as their own. Stalking is a serious crime. Take legal action to protect yourself; don't wait until it's too late. Document everything you can when the stalker is near, such as what he is wearing, what was said, location, time, date and who else was there. If you are being stalked, notify the police.

Business Trips and Conventions: Conventions are known hot spots for scams, cons, robbery and sexual assault. Be aware of strangers and an over friendly person. Remove your name badge immediately after your meetings. Make it your rule to meet business partners and associates at a busy public location such as a hotel lobby or restaurant. Never meet at someone's room or vehicle. Keep it professional even when away from the office.

On business trips you may find yourself eating alone so take precautions when leaving the restaurant. Be sure you're not being followed back to your hotel or vehicle. If you are driving, follow the suggestions given in the automobile safety chapter.

Vacation Safety In the States

Travel Safety: Don't wing your trip. Plan before you leave and have a map; get familiar with the area you are traveling to. Not all states have this safety measure, but you can call the highway patrol in the state you will travel to and ask for the emergency cell phone codes for that area. Example: PA Highway Patrol is 911, # 77 for the State Highway emergency in Virginia, *55 for Oklahoma Highway

Patrol, *999 for Wisconsin. Those codes come in handy if you have vehicle trouble or are faced with an emergency.

Before leaving, have your mechanic check your vehicle fluids, oil and filter, battery, tire pressure, wheel alignment, windshield wipers, maintenance tune-up, lights, air conditioning or heater. Make sure your vehicle is in excellent running condition before you leave for your trip.

If you are renting a vehicle ask that all markings identifying it as a rental be removed. When you are in your new destination, don't look like a tourist; try to blend in. Be inconspicuous when reading a map; don't make it obvious. Fold the map and hold it on top of a magazine or book. That way your not alerting others that you're a tourist and / or lost. If you are lost, ask a family, a mother with kids, or someone in authority for directions.

Tourists and sight-seekers are always a target for criminal acts. Keep safety in mind at all times and don't let your guard down. As vacationers, we have a tendency to lower our guard and feel safe. Every city has its trouble spots, so ask the police or hotel managers about locations to avoid. If you are traveling with others, stay together as a group. Don't leave anyone alone or behind at a public restroom, restaurant, store, bar... not everyone is looking out for your safety.

Airport, Subway and Train Station safety: For parents traveling with children, don't allow your kids to run around or play hide and seek under the seats. It is all too easy for a child to get lost. Keep them in your sight at all times. Escort your children to the restroom; you have no idea who is in that restroom. Many airports offer a family restroom.

Be cautious of overly friendly people. Criminals sometimes have drugged food and drinks, offering it to fellow passengers, then assaulting and / or robbing them. Never accept anything from anyone at the airport or a train station. Avoid small talk and never discuss your personal or travel plans with a stranger. Do not put your name and home address on your luggage. Use your business address and tag it inside of your luggage. If your luggage falls into the wrong hands you may be coming home to a burglarized house. When riding a train, lock your compartment. If you plan on sleeping, secure your luggage to yourself and, if possible, lay on top of it.

Never ask someone who you maybe sitting near to watch your luggage while you use the restroom or go for a snack. Always keep your belongings with you and in sight. Expensive luggage is a target to criminals. Secure duct tape on or around your luggage. It is unappealing but it aids in two ways: it will let you know if someone has tampered with your luggage, and you will be able to recognize it easily. Get to baggage claim area as soon as possible if your luggage continues to go around on the belt someone else can easily walk off with it or go through it with out your knowledge. Something I learned the hard way is when traveling with someone else spilt your clothes between the two suitcases in case your luggage gets lost. That way you at least have a few of your belongings until the airport recovers your luggage. Keep your credit cards, ATM card and cash in a safe place, typically on you, until you reach your hotel or destination. When you arrive at the hotel use the hotel safe to secure your credit cards, extra medicine and expensive jewelry. Close and lock your room door securely whenever you are in the room. Check the sliding glass doors, windows and any connecting room doors to see that they are locked. Don't answer the door of your room without verifying whom it is. If they claim to be hotel staff, call the front desk and ask questions. For what purpose do they need access to your room? Many people have been hurt and / or robbed by hotel imposters.

Never leave your room key needlessly displayed, such as near the pool, on a restaurant table, or on a counter. They can be easily stolen. When heading out, only take what credit cards and money you would need in a special travel pouch that you wear around your neck or under your clothes. This is a safe way to keep your money and cards with you. Purchase them at AAA, Wal-Mart, travel stores and luggage shops. Keep emergency cash hidden in a separate place other than your purse or wallet, and don't carry all your money with you. Use credit cards, ATM cards or travelers checks; you can report your card stolen and immediately cancel it. Be sure to have a copy of your toll free credit card number so you can easily call to report the stolen card. When returning to your hotel in the evening, use the main entrance of the hotel. If you notice any suspicious activity, report it to hotel management.

When enjoying yourself at public restaurants, fairs, and clubs, keep your drink in sight at all times. Simply keep your hand over your glass in a relaxed manner. If you leave your drink to go to the dance floor, the restroom, or to visit someone at another table, don't leave your drink unattended. Keep it with you or buy a new drink when you return to your table. An unattended drink could be drugged without your knowledge, putting you at extreme risk. A good strategy is to make sure you have time to finish most of your drink before you leave the table. Then you won't have to feel like you will offend your companions when you come back by ordering a new drink.

Never, under any circumstances, leave an intoxicated friend alone or allow them to leave with someone they just met recently or that night. Many women have been attacked and/or killed by this would-be new friend. Your friend who has had too much to drink is unable to make a responsible decision. It is up to you and others to step in and keep them safe. Be a true friend. Intervene; do not allow them to leave with someone they just met or don't really know well. Be there logic for them because you may just save them from harm.

When walking during the day or evening, stay on well-lit busy streets. Do not take short cuts or alleys. Stay with others because there is safety in numbers.

Tips for your home while you are away: Remember to have your mail held for you at your local post office. Ask a neighbor to collect any newspapers or mailings that may be left at your front door. I suggest that you ask a neighbor to place trash bags or a can out on trash day and to park their vehicle in your driveway for a while. It gives the impression that someone is home. Leave your window shades and blinds the way you would if you were home. Drawn shades can actually protect the thief as he goes through your house. Lights are a deterrent to a burglar who is looking for an empty house, so illuminate entrances and walkways. You can purchase screw-in light controls or a light sensor for your lights to be used inside or outside of your home at hardware stores. They turn lights on at dusk and off at dawn; they are a great addition to your safety and security. Have a few of your lights inside the house programmed on timers to come on and off as if someone where truly home, such as the kitchen light, then the family room light, a hallway light and the bedroom. Program a radio or television to turn on and off periodically. Turn your phone ringers on low or off so if someone is prowling outside your house they will not hear that someone is not answering the phone, which can be a sure sign that you're not home. If you have a home security system, arm it. Call your provider and let them know your date of departure and return date. Contact your local police department and ask them to check on your house periodically.

VACATIONS ABROAD

Taking a trip without proper planning is ill advised. You need to understand where you are going and seek advice and travel advisories. Going out of the country unprepared can also make for a disappointing trip. Avoid mishaps by taking the time to plan.

Before leaving, confirm your hotel and ask the hotel clerk about the weather forecast, or check online at www.weather.com. Confirm your travel plans and be sure you reserved rooms and arranged for transportation. In Europe, for instance, you will need to purchase electrical receptors for your American electrical gadgets. Make sure you understand how you are going to get from one place to the other. Are you going to take a cab, the tube, buses or shuttle? Sometimes it is more advisable to take a cab because you won't have to walk in an unknown location. How much cash will you need? Do you have sufficient traveler's checks and a credit card? It is advisable to notify your bank and your credit card companies that you are going out of the country if you plan on using your bankcard and credit cards.

Learn their phone systems. Know how the emergency calls work and how to make out of the country calls. Know where the US Embassy is located. Become familiar with the laws of the country that you will be traveling to.

U.S. Embassy / Consulate http://travel.state.gov/travel/tips/embassies/embassies_1214.html.

Be inconspicuous when reading a map; don't make it obvious. Fold the map and hold it on top of a magazine or book. That way you're not alerting others that you're a tourist or lost. Tourists and sight-seekers are always a target for criminal acts. Keep safety in mind at all times and don't let your guard down.

Don't look like a tourist; try to conform to the local dress. In many countries such as Europe, blue jeans are a true give away that you are American. Jeans are expensive in other countries. The norm would be to wear khakis or Dockers. Don't wear expensive jewelry; dress conservatively. You do not want to draw the wrong type of attention to yourself. Criminals may single you out because they find your clothing offensive because of their culture. Respect the country's values and customs. Do not be loud, rude or vulgar. Keep safety in mind wherever you travel, and don't let your guard down. When you get too relaxed, that's when trouble will strike and you will be caught off guard. Pick-pocketing occurs everywhere, so keep your wallet in your front pants pocket. Carry your money and cards in a secure traveler's wallet that fits snugly around your waist under your clothes or around your neck. If traveling with others, stay together as a group. Don't leave anyone alone or behind. Never allow someone in your group to leave with locals that they have just met. Many criminals look for naïve visitors, the over joyous visitor that is in the relaxed state of mind. Their thinking is "Hey, I am a visitor here nothing is going to happen to me!" Criminals will take advantage of you. Don't allow this to happen to anyone in your group.

Remember, a criminal is not a dirty, smelly, unkempt person. Criminals are just like everyone else. They may appear friendly, likeable, attractive, well-spoken, charming, and funny. You can enjoy yourself on vacation while maintaining safe habits.

Just as in the states, never accept anything from anyone at the airport, subway or train station. Allow for extra time at the airports. Some foreign airports, even the big international airports will make you empty your entire contents in your suitcases and search them. This procedure is frequently done in Europe. When going through customs, only answer their questions. Do not small talk or make jokes. The customs officer will view this as nervousness on your part and you may cause suspicion. You will be pulled to the side. You, everyone in your group will be searched. This is a time consuming process so don't be nervous. Be calm and only speak when spoken to. Customs officers are doing their jobs to keep everyone safe.

Do not travel with any illegal substances. A foreign jail is definitely not fun. Follow all local and countrywide laws. When traveling, use your business address on all your luggage, not your home address. Place your name on the inside of your luggage. Expensive luggage is a target to criminals so consider purchasing sturdy ordinary looking luggage, not a set that draws attention. Get to baggage claim area as soon as possible if your luggage continues to go around on the belt someone can easily walk off with it or go through it with out your knowledge. Keep your passport, credit cards, ATM card and cash in a safe place, such as the hotel safe or in a special travel pouch that you wear around your neck or under your clothes. You can purchase travel pouches at AAA, Wal-Mart, travel stores and luggage shops. Keep emergency cash hidden in a separate place other than your purse or wallet and don't carry all your money with you. Use credit cards or ATM cards or travelers checks; you can report your card stolen and immediately cancel it. Keep valuables and medicine with you when you are traveling. Have your medical card with you for any medical emergency that arises. Have extra medicine in your suitcase and with you at all times. Notify your doctor that you are going out of the country in case you need a quick refill. Keep all medicines in a clear bag in the original container. If you are searched and your medicines are not labeled they will be confiscated. Leave your itinerary and a copy of your passport with a family member or close friend back home in case of an emergency. Enjoy other countries and cultures but use common sense. Stay alert and be wise, because not every one is looking out for your best interest. They may be looking out for themselves.

Have your passport ready when driving through customs. For instance, Americans going into Canada or Mexico: only answer the customs officer's questions. Do not make small talk or joke. The customs officer will view this as nervousness on your part and you may cause suspicion. You will be pulled to the side. You, plus everyone in the vehicle and your vehicle will be searched. This is a time consuming process so don't be nervous or disrespectful; be calm, and only speak when spoken to. Give short direct answers. Customs officers are doing their jobs to keep everyone safe.

When traveling abroad for an extended time period, get an International Driving Permit and bring your US drivers license even if you're not planning to drive. Should you need to communicate with foreign authorities, this recognizable form of identification can help you get on your way more quickly. TripAdvisory.com and the US Dept of State will give you updates for each country. Those sites offer information on travel warnings, health conditions, and emergency services, crime, currency exchange and other updated information. Another resource you might want to try would be travel magazines.

Tips for your home while you are away: Remember to have your mail held for you at your local post office. Ask a neighbor to collect any newspapers or mailings that may be left at your door. I hire a neighbor's child for that job. I also suggest that you ask a neighbor to place trash bags or a can out on trash day and to park their vehicle in your driveway for a while. It gives the impression that someone is home. Leave your window shades and blinds the way you would if you where home. Drawn shades can actually protect the thief as he goes through your house. Lights are a deterrent to a burglar who is looking for an empty house so illuminate entrances and walkways. You can purchase screw-in light controls or a light sensor for your lights to be used inside or outside of your home at hardware stores. They turn lights on at dusk and off at dawn, and are a great addition to your safety and security. Have a few of your lights inside the house programmed on timers to come on and off as if someone where truly home such as the kitchen light, then the family room light, a hallway light, and then the bedroom. Program a radio or television to turn on and off periodically. Turn your phone ringers on low or off so if someone is prowling outside your house they will not hear that someone is not answering the phone a sure sign that your not home. If you have a home security system, arm it. Call your provider to let them know your date of departure and return date. Contact your local police department and ask them to check on your house periodically.

Part III

Exercise

Exercise promotes physical and psychological benefits. If you look and feel good about yourself, you'll project more confidence and have greater self-esteem. Most criminals look for vulnerable targets. Projecting confidence makes you less of a target.

If you exercise, you might live longer independently, and with a better quality of life. Simply walking every day for 20 minutes helps your strength and gains endurance to make every day duties easier on your body. Weight training builds your bones keeping them strong and your body healthy. Stretching your muscles promotes the health of your tendons and ligaments. It increases your flexibility, improves balance and helps to prevent injury. Doing something active is healthier than doing nothing at all! Think healthy so you can be the best you can be!

Before starting any exercise regimen get the approval from your doctor.

Mental Techniques

Courage and Associates does not guarantee anyone's safety, nor foresee how you will be attacked.

Your first reaction should always be to retreat to safety, if you can. Use the self-defense techniques as a last option.

The techniques discussed in *Courage, You've Got It* are to be used if you are in fear for your life! Take the techniques seriously. They can cause temporary or permanent bodily damage possibly leading to death if executed properly.

You must practice the techniques to lock them into your muscle memory. When you are scared it is your muscle memory that takes over, not your brain.

SO PRACTICE – PRACTICE – PRACTICE

These survival techniques are effective and easy to learn and remember. You do not need agility or strength because strength against strength is ineffective. Spirit and attitude are more important than size and strength. The size and strength of the attacker does not matter. It's how you respond that counts.

When practicing with a partner, start slowly, then more rapidly. (Practice using your left and right side.) Remember to view your attacker as a target and not as a person. Look at your target when striking; try to place your strike precisely on the target. If you are striking the knee with a sidekick, look at the knee, don't look at your attackers face. The side of your foot should be aiming directly on the attacker's knee; that is your target. When doing a finger jab to the eyes, look at the eyes; they are your target.

Yell to keep yourself breathing. Many people will hold their breath, so be sure to check your breathing as you practice your techniques. Breathing keeps your muscles relaxed and when your muscles are relaxed you will deliver more power and force to your target. The goal is to deliver full force to the target! When striking, step into the assailant going towards him with full impact, stepping into the strike.

There are no excuses for not practicing. You do not need a partner to practice; just visualize your attacker in different attack scenarios and do your techniques. Move slowly then more rapidly with your strikes. Effective techniques are more important than speed. Learning slowly can mean learning more thoroughly. Speed is not as important as learning your strike properly. Speed will come in time.

Practice in the dark and in tight areas, in different weather conditions and different ground surfaces. Practice wearing different outfits and shoes. If wearing a short or long skirt it might restrict your kicks so you will have to pull it up slightly to get the best range for your technique.

You will find you my have to alter your techniques under certain circumstances.

The element of surprise is to your advantage in self-defense. You should never reveal or brag to co-workers or friends that you know self-defense, because doing so is a negative. **Keep your self-defense knowledge to yourself** and have it as your own quiet source to use to minimize confrontations or assault. Comply then surprise! Use it when he least expects it and never telegraph your moves. Wait until the last second then explode, striking hard and fast on your target. Your voice is a great distraction. If your attacker tells you not to scream, as long as he does not have a weapon pointed at you, yell as loud as you can. Do not listen to your attackers commands. Yelling may be just enough to scare him off. It also shows that you are not going down without a fight. Remember even if you're in a public place and other people are around, yelling doesn't mean someone is going to come to your rescue. Unfortunately, too many citizens don't have courage. They will not interfere and help. They choose to look the other way due to lack of courage. That is why it is important for everyone to know how to physically defend themselves against a life threatening assault. When in fear for your life, take the measures to survive.

Everyone should work on having civil courage. Having civil courage does not mean getting physically involved in a threatening situation. You can be safe and call 911 from a distance. Yell that you need someone to call 911. Getting other people to see what is going on is another way to draw attention to the situation. I recently heard on the news of a young teenager who severely beat up a 90 year old man as he was getting into his car; standing just a few feet away were a group of young men and women who stood there, glancing over at the commotion but did absolutely nothing to help or get help for that man. Needless to say the felonious teenager drove off with his car, and the elderly man sustained serious injuries from that attack. In my opinion those young adults that witnessed this crime are cowards and should be held responsible in some way or another.

PHYSICAL TECHNIQUES

FINGER BREAK - Hook onto any finger or thumb securely. Using a quick forceful motion pull backwards on the finger or thumb, bending the finger towards the top of the hand. The bones on the hand are soft and break with little force. If your assailant has a broken finger he will not be able to hold onto you or a weapon as well.

You can also tear the webbing between the fingers by holding onto two fingers and pulling outwardly. This causes excruciating pain.

FOUR-FINGER EYE JAB - (four is better than two.) Jab all four fingers of one hand into the eyes of your assailant. This strike disrupts his vision and ability to attack you. Twisting at your waist keeping your elbow close to the body as you step forward lunging at your target, the eyes. This strike requires very little force, a quick short jab. Shoot your arm out and back quickly. This strike will cause temporary or permanent blindness, severe pain and shock. The assailant will raise his hands to comfort his eyes allowing you the opportunity to retreat to safety or to follow through with another strike. Practice on a pillow or a mannequin head. You can purchase mannequins at a Halloween store or a beauty supply shop.

FIST - roll your fingers up into the palm of your hand, keeping your thumb in front. Do not enclose it under your fingers or have your thumb on the side near your forefinger. You have a high possibility of breaking your thumb in those two locations. Do not bend your wrist, keep your hand, wrist and forearm straight.

HAMMER FIST – This can go any where on the body. You can strike up, down, or across. For instance, if you strike the nose it will result in a stunning pain to the face; the nose most likely will bleed and the eyes may begin to water, allowing you to retreat to safety or follow through with another strike. A powerful strike to the head can result in shock to unconsciousness. Practice a hammer fist by swinging into a pillow or a hand-held target. Strike with the meaty portion of your hand.

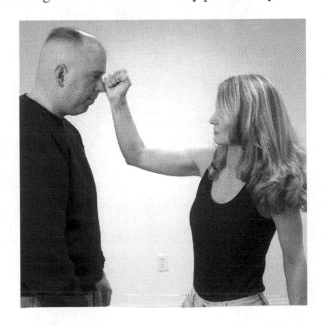

Hammer fist into the groin – This strike is most effective by a low swinging hammer fist, coming from underneath the testicles. Striking the groin causes severe pain, nausea, vomiting, and shortness of breath. The assailant may double over, allowing you to follow through with a hammer fist to the back of their head. If you strike hard enough you will push the testicles up inside the assailant's cavity, causing true pain and possible death if he does not receive medical attention. What transpires is, the blood flow gets cut off and stops flowing through his body causing serious problems to occur.

Hammer fist to the back of the head – Aim for the soft spot where the neck and head meet. These are the first seven vertebrae of the spinal column, and they control the nerve impulses from the brain to the body. This strike can cause shock, unconsciousness, a broken neck, coma and death depending on the force of your strike.

Palm heel strike to the side of the jaw – Bend the wrist so your palm is exposed facing upwards and fingers bent. You should strike up and forward into the side of the assailants jaw. Keep your elbow close to your body. Twist your body into the move, stepping forward with the same leg and arm you're striking with. Example, if you're striking with your right arm, step forward with your right leg, twisting at your waist. This strike jars the head & snaps it back, possibly causing them to bite their tongue or lip, and perhaps chipping a tooth. This strike also puts the attacker off balance. A heavy blow could result in whiplash to the neck, a broken jaw, concussion and unconsciousness. Practice on a small pillow held high enough to imitate someone's jaw height. Or use small hand-held targets, holding them at an angle.

SIDEKICK TO THE KNEE – Bring your leg up to knee level. You're not doing a high kick, but a low kick. You're shooting your leg straight out with your eyes focused on the assailants knee. Shoot your leg out striking the knee, and bring your leg back. Keep your foot horizontal (parallel) with the ground. Your supporting leg will be slightly bent. Keep your hands close to your body, one at chest level and the other near your head but not blocking your vision. If you can hold onto the attacker, do so and pull them in as you strike the knee.

The knee is a very weak joint. Striking the knee will tear ligaments causing swelling and severe pain. A forceful strike will immobilize the assailant, bringing him down to the ground in agonizing pain. Practice the sidekick by holding onto a couch, wall, or countertop. Bring your leg up to the side and shoot it out quickly, pretending you're in position with the assailant and keeping your eyes focused on the location of the assailant's knee. Bring your leg back and repeat on the other leg.

KNEE STRIKE INTO THE GROIN – Grasp tightly onto the assailant for your stability. You may dig into his skin or clothing. Hold onto his hair if necessary. Angle your head to the side, not directly in front of his. When you strike him he will lean forward with his upper body potentially hitting you in the head. Bring one of your legs back. Smash forcefully into the groin repeatedly with your knee. Be sure to hold onto him so you don't fall.

Striking the groin causes severe pain, nausea, vomiting, and shortness of breath. The assailant may double over, allowing you to follow through with a hammer fist to the back of their head. Practice by pretending someone grabbed you from the front, your arms are pinned to your side. Hook onto him and knee strike two to three times. Be sure to move your upper body to the side.

Kidnapping, date rape, sexual assault, domestic violence and any form of physical assault is a close encounter between you and the attacker. You want to stay in close to your assailant to get the best result from your techniques. It sounds unnatural, but as women you want to stay in close.

ASSAILANT GRABS YOUR WRIST FORCING YOU TO GO WITH HIM - Do not resist. Go with the flow as you step forward with the same side he grabbed you on. Flip your wrist up, palm facing upwards. Hook onto the assailant's finger, quickly and forcefully breaking it. Immediately lunge forward executing a four-finger eye jab with either hand.

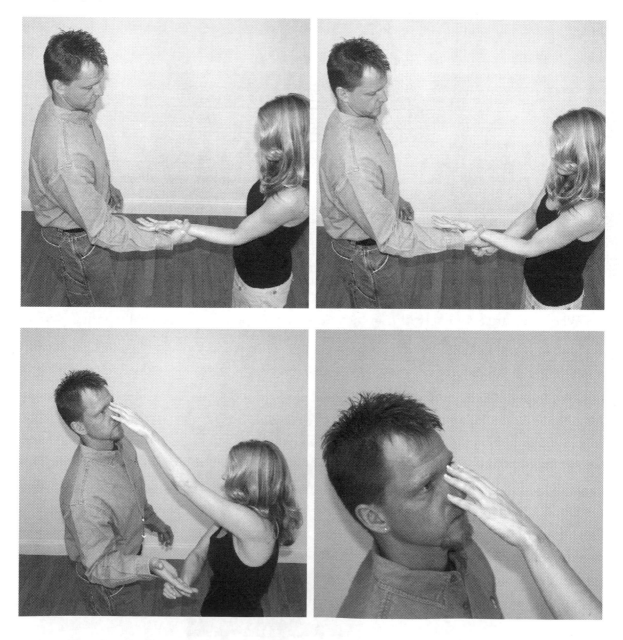

ASSAILANT GRABS YOUR WRIST FORCING YOU TO GO WITH HIM – Make a fist with the hand he grabbed. With a quick snapping motion bring your fisted hand up to your shoulder as you continue stepping forward. With a sudden thrust of your four-finger eye jab with the opposite hand into the attackers eyes or palm heel strike into the side of the jaw.

Simplifying it: Snap out with your fisted hand, lunge forward and eye jab.

Note: Align the entire side of your body as you do your technique. Example: If grabbed on the left wrist be sure your left foot is forward when you break free from the wrist grab. Aligning your entire side of your body gives you more power.

WRIST GRAB - If this is a kidnapping or threatening situation you must follow through with a four-finger eye jab to the attackers eyes. If the assailant is wearing glasses use a palm heel strike to the side of the jaw. *Note: that in most kidnapping situations, the assailant will threaten you verbally. Do not be shocked by what he says. You want to physically respond to your threat and not digest his words.*

ASSAILANT GRABS YOUR WRIST AS YOUR BOTH STANDING SIDE BY SIDE HE IS THREATENING YOU VERBALLY - Hook onto his fingers bending them backwards forcefully hyper extending the attackers hand. Use your other hand to reinforce your hold. Straighten up his wrist causing extreme pain. Hold on to his hand and knee strike with the leg closest to your attacker.

ASSAILANT GRABS YOU IN A CROSS OVER MANNER – your palms are face to face. Make a fist with the arm he grabbed. Bring your arm up quickly and forcefully as you step forward with the same side of the wrist that was grabbed. Do a four-finger eye jab with the other arm. OR a palm heel strike to the side of the jaw. You are breaking free between the thumb and fingers.

Simplifying it: Snap out with your fisted hand, aligning that side of your body, then eye jab.

ASSAILANT GRABS YOU IN A CROSS OVER MANNER – hook your hand on top of his in a quick inward motion. Place your other hand on top of his to lock in place. Bend arm downward, controlling him. This technique could be used on someone you do not want to hurt. It puts you in control with compliance on the other person's part. If it turns serious do a palm heel strike to the face.

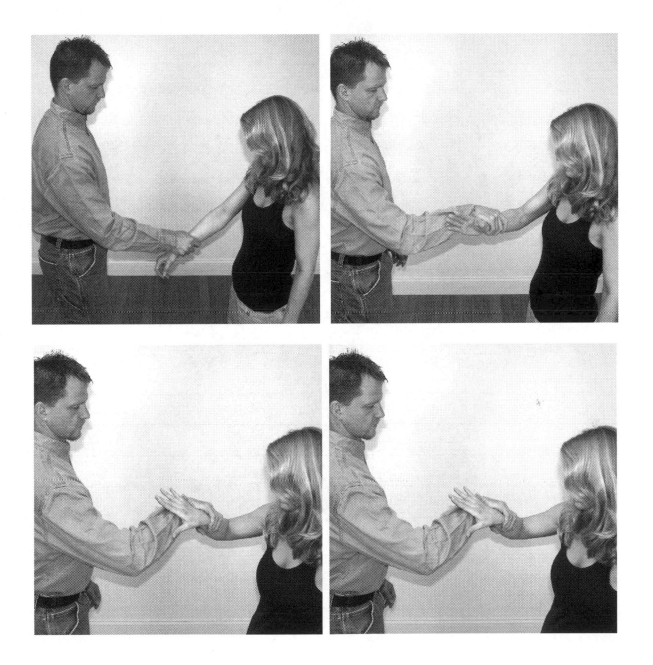

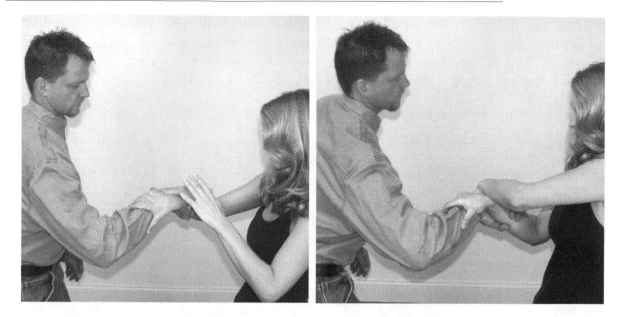

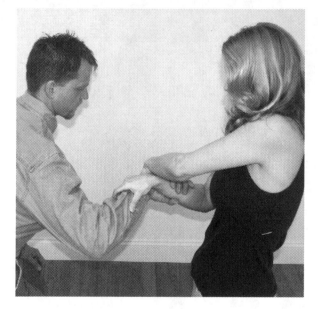

ASSAILANT GRABS BOTH YOUR WRISTS HOLDING THEM CLOSE TO YOUR SHOULDERS - Immediately knee strike into the groin, leaning your upper body to one side to avoid being struck by his head.

ASSAILANT GRABS BOTH YOUR WRISTS HOLDING THEM CLOSE TO YOUR HIPS - He squeezes you in tightly against his body. Grab his testicles and squeeze or knee strike into the groin. Moving your head to the side.

GRABBED BY ATTACKER ON WRIST AND NEAR THE ELBOW LOCKING YOUR ARM – Immediately eye jab with your free hand; forearm strike into the side of the neck. Another choice is to do a knee strike or a low hammer fist into the groin.

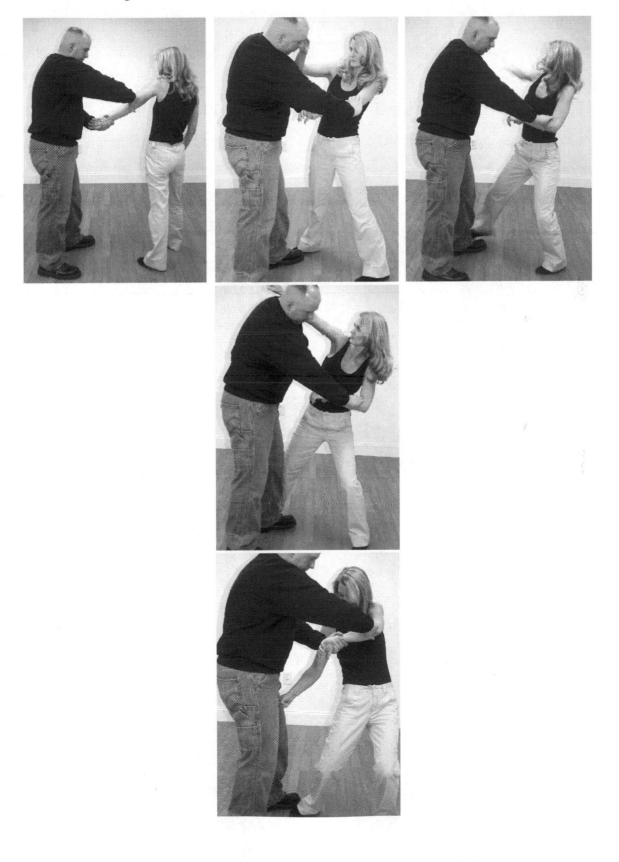

LAPEL HOLD BY ONE HAND – Place the opposite hand that the assailant grabbed you with on top of the assailant's hand pressing both hands into your chest. With your free arm form an L. Step into the assailant with the same leg that your arm is raised in the L shape, and quickly twist your entire body, striking the assailants elbow with a forceful elbow strike, keeping a tight hold with the other hand. You are not coming up and down on the elbow, you are coming straight across in a smooth, forceful straight line. You will hit the assailant's elbow with the side of your elbow. This technique will break the elbow and the wrist. The shoulder will pop out of place. Step and twist your entire body into the strike.

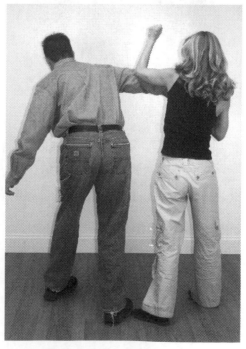

TWO HAND LAPEL GRAB – Bring your arms up and hold onto his arms, knee strike into the groin or do a low swinging hammer fist into the groin. Lean your upper body to the side so his upper body does not hit you. You could also eye jab.

TWO HAND LAPEL GRAB BEING HELD AGAINST THE WALL – twist your entire body to one side, quickly punching downward right below the belly button. If he is wearing a belt, punch under the belt. OR hook onto attackers arms and lean your upper body to one side and knee strike repeatedly into the groin.

SHOULDER GRAB FROM THE LEFT OR RIGHT SIDE - Raising the arm of the same side attacker is holding. Simultaneously step backwards into the attacker. Come around quickly with your other arm and eye jab, palm heel strike or throat strike. *NOTE: A throat strike can be lethal. Use only if you're in fear for your life.*

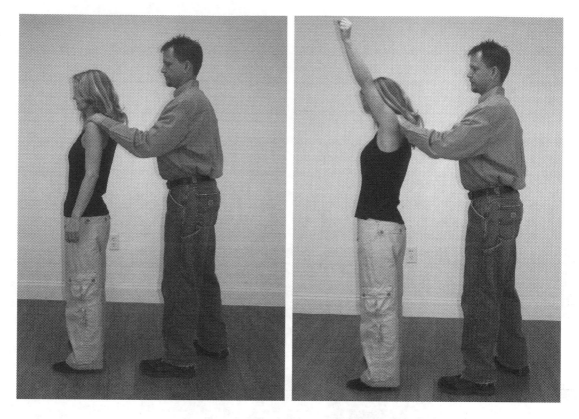

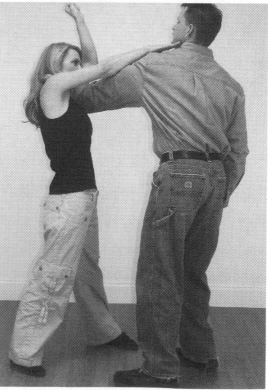

SHOULDER GRAB FROM THE CENTER OF YOUR BACK – Raise your arm straight up, twisting into the attacker. Do a low swinging hammer fist into groin with your other hand. *OR* Raise your arm, twisting into attacker with your other arm eye jab, palm heel strike or throat strike.

ASSAILANT GRABS YOUR CLOTHES FROM THE SIDE OR BACK – turn slightly to face him. Using your hand that is closest to him hammer fist into his groin OR using your hand farthest from him hammer fist into his face. You must do this strike quickly because he will see it coming if you project what your intending to do. So you must practice and be quick, turn and strike at that same time.

BEAR HUG FROM THE FRONT; YOUR ARMS ARE PINNED – Hook onto assailant and knee strike into the groin. Lean your upper body to the side so his upper body will not hit you as you strike into the groin.

BEAR HUG FROM THE FRONT; YOU'RE BEING LIFTED OFF THE GROUND – Hook onto the assailant and do a forceful upward knee strike into the groin OR bite hard into the shoulder then eye jab.

YOUR NATURAL REACTION IN A PINNED POSITION IS TO PUSH YOUR ASSAILANT AWAY FROM YOU! YOU WANT TO KEEP HIM IN CLOSE FOR YOUR COUNTER TECHNIQUES; YOU WILL GET THE MOST BENEFIT OUT OF YOUR TECHNIQUES BY STAYING IN CLOSE

BEAR HUG FROM THE BACK; YOUR ARMS ARE PINNED - Foot stomp or shin scrape, swing hips out without moving your feet, immediately hammer fist the groin two or three times. Without hesitation bring the same striking hand up and grab a finger. Pull the finger outward breaking it with a quick jerking motion as you begin to step out from the hold. Taking the path of least resistance. *Stepping to the side of the assailant, staying close to him and continue holding onto his finger. Sidekick into his knee. Be sure to rotate your hips before you do a sidekick. *When stepping out, do not step to far out to the side of the assailant stay in close.

Simplifying it: foot stomp, hammer fist to groin, finger break, step out and break knee.

BEAR HUG FROM THE BACK YOUR ARMS ARE FREE — break finger with a quick jerking motion as you begin to step out from the hold. Hold onto his finger, step out but stay close to the assailant and sidekick into his knee.

BEAR HUG FROM THE BACK YOUR ARMS ARE PINNED AND YOUR BEING LIFTED OFF THE GROUND – If you can, immediately heel strike into the groin. OR Hook onto a finger and forcefully break it. Twist facing assailant and quickly eye jab or palm heel strike to the side of the jaw.

CHOKE HOLD FROM THE FRONT – (Statue of Liberty) hold your arm straight up as if your arm was a baseball bat. Keep your arm as close to your ear as you can. Keep your elbow locked. Step towards your attacker with the leg of the same side as your arm that is raised. Pivoting on the other leg keeping your arm straight up as you are stepping half way around your assailant. At this point your back will be towards the assailant. Quickly bring your arm down to your side bending at the elbow. This locks the assailant's hands under your arm, without hesitation follow through with a forearm strike to the assailant's neck or an elbow strike to the assailants face with the same hand that you were holding straight up. You could also twist into him and finger jab the eyes with the outside hand.

Additional strikes would be to hook onto him with the same hand as you elbowed into his face or did the forearm strike with. Hook him by grabbing his arm after your strike, hold onto him for stability and break his knee or do a groin strike. Keep your eyes focused on the target.

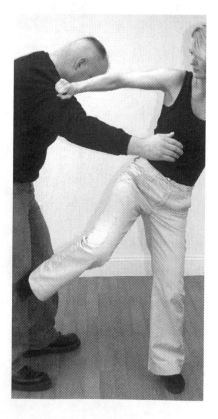

CHOKE HOLD FROM THE BACK – (Statue of Liberty) hold your arm straight up as if your arm was a baseball bat. Keep your arm as close to your ear as possible and have your elbow locked. Twist into your assailant quickly, stepping with the same side that you raised your arm with. Immediately eye jab or palm heel strike into the side of the jaw with your other arm.

Choke hold from the back - Grab his fingers on both hands with your hands, quickly and forcefully spread apart his fingers; simultaneously bend slightly forward with your upper body, twist into him and hammer fist into groin, eye jab or palm heel strike.

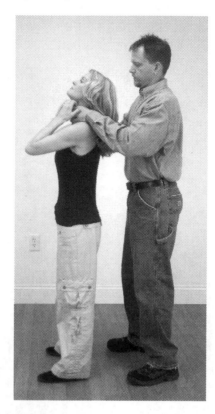

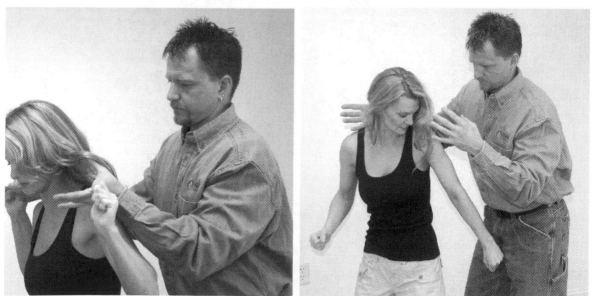

CHOKE HOLD FROM THE BACK - Grab his fingers on both hands with both of your hands, quickly and forcefully spread apart his fingers; hold onto one of his fingers letting go of the other hand. Twist out slightly, staying in close, holding onto him for stability. Do a sidekick to his knee. Kicking with the leg closest to him, not your leg that is on the outside. Never cross your legs one over the other to kick.

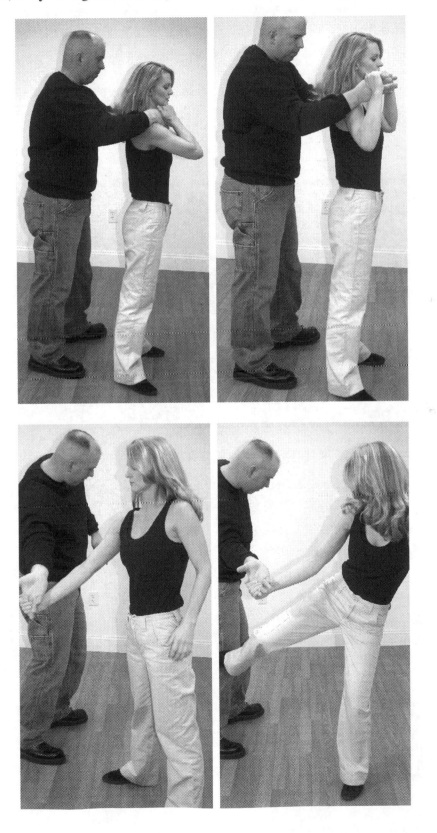

THROAT CHOKE FROM THE REAR; ASSAILANTS ARM IS STRAIGHT ACROSS YOUR AIRWAY, ONE ARM IS PINNED BEHIND YOUR BACK – When your air way is being cut off you only have a few seconds before you start to panic. Chances are if you wait to long, you may pass out. To avoid that from occurring open your airway by turning your head into the crease of his elbow. Foot stomp or shin scrape, slide hips out without moving your feet, immediately hammer fist the groin two or three times. Bring the same striking hand up and grab a finger. Pull the finger outward, breaking it with a quick jerking motion as you begin to step out from the hold. Stepping to the side of the assailant, hold onto his finger and sidekick into his knee.

Simplifying it: Open your airway by bringing your face towards the elbow, foot stomp, hammer fist to groin, finger break, break knee.

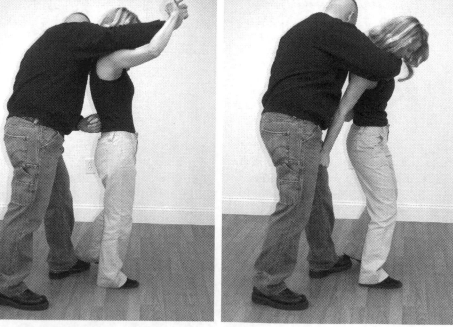

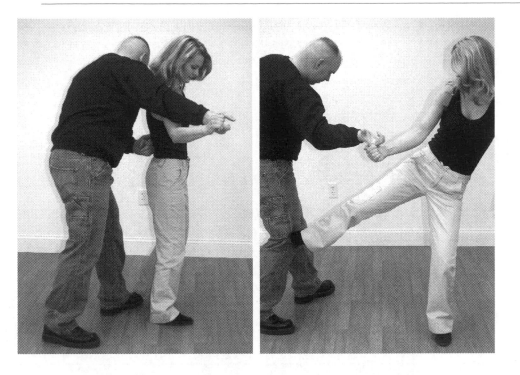

THROAT CHOKE FROM THE REAR; ASSAILANTS ELBOW IS BENT (YOUR AIRWAY IS OPEN) - foot stomp or shin scrape, swing your hips out without moving your feet. Immediately hammer fist the groin two or three times. Bring the same striking hand up and grab a finger. Pull the finger outward breaking it with a quick jerking motion as you begin to step out from the hold. Taking the path of least resistance. Stepping to the side of the assailant, hold on to his finger and sidekick into his knee.

Simplifying it: foot stomp, hammer fist to groin, finger break, break knee. Grabbed from behind, assailant covers your mouth and pins one arm behind your back - Do a hammer fist into the groin. As he releases you could follow through with a hammer fist to the back of the skull.

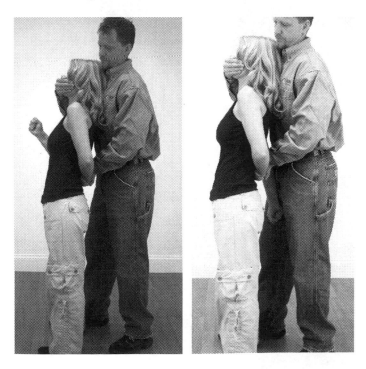

GRABBED FROM BEHIND, ASSAILANT COVERS YOUR MOUTH AND PINS ONE ARM BEHIND YOUR BACK — grab one of his fingers forcefully bend it backwards, step out slightly, staying in close and holding on to the finger and side kick the knee.

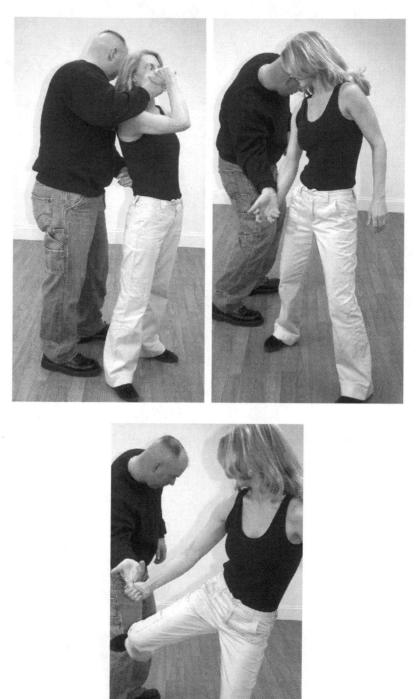

HAIR GRABBED FROM THE BACK AND YOUR BEING DRAGGED - Grab their wrist with your hand farthest from assailant. Hold your hand as close to his hand and push down on your scalp. Do not pull away from him. As your walking hammer fist, two or three times into the groin with the hand closest to him. *OR* Kick as hard as you can into his shin or stomp on his instep. When he loosens his grip on your hair, strike the eyes or groin.

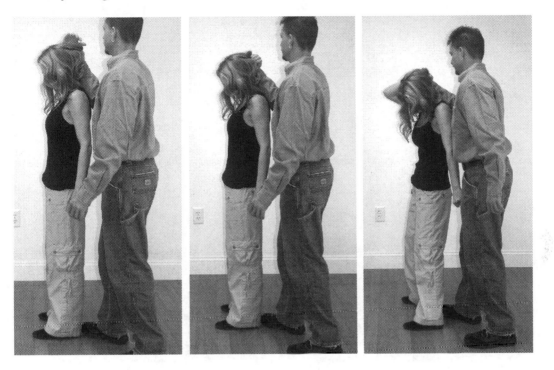

HAIR GRABBED FROM THE SIDE – Strike with the arm closest to assailant with a straight forearm strike across assailants throat / neck. Simultaneously as you strike place your leg closest to the assailant behind his leg. Your strike will cause him to be off balance and fall backwards.

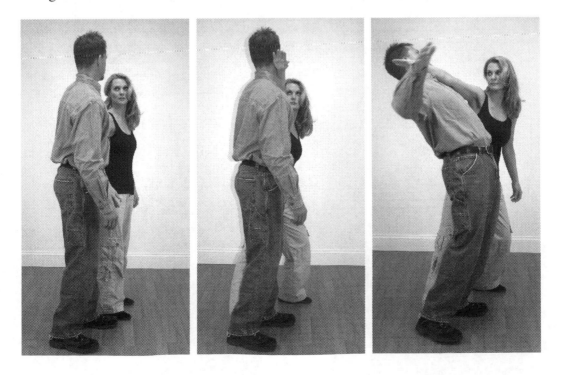

SITTING ON A BENCH, SOMEONE SITTING NEXT TO YOU IS HARASSING YOU AND PURPOSELY TOUCHES YOUR LEG – hook onto their finger or hand and apply pressure by bending it backwards. Verbalize to them that you wish to be left alone. If he doesn't leave, you should, and get to a safe place.

SITTING ON A BENCH, SOMEONE UNINVITED PUTS HIS HAND AROUND YOUR SHOULDER AND SQUEEZES AS HE THREATENS YOU – grab one of his fingers with your arm that is on the same side of his fingers and finger break. Quickly follow through with a forceful eye jab OR twist towards assailant and grab his groin; squeeze and twist the testicles.

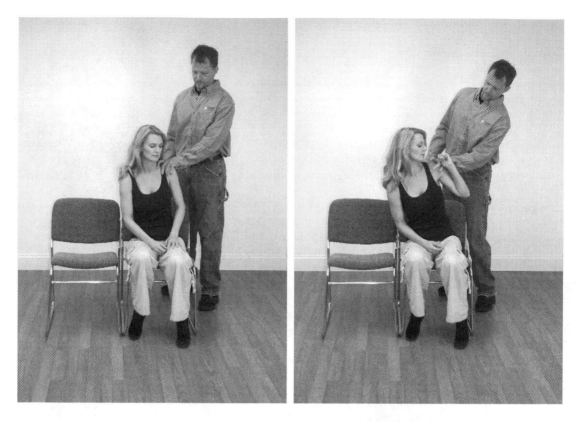

SITTING ON A BENCH, SOMEONE UNINVITED PUTS HIS HAND AROUND YOUR SHOULDER AND SQUEEZES AS HE THREATENS YOU – use your opposite hand secure assailants hand by placing your thumb on top and between the middle knuckles. Twist assailant's hand so his palm will be facing upwards. With your other hand secure and apply pressure bending his wrist towards him.

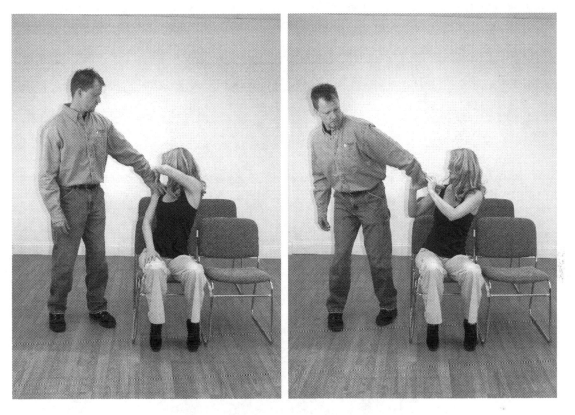

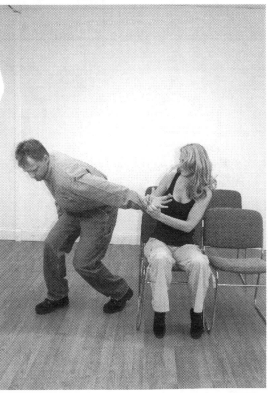

SITTING ON A BENCH OR ON A BUS, SOMEONE STANDING NEXT TO YOU IS PHYSICALLY HARASSING YOU – After your first verbal warning if he touches you again, punch him in the *common peroneal nerve with the hand closest to him or grab their hand and bend it backwards. Verbalize loudly that you do not appreciate him touching you inappropriately. You want to speak calmly yet in a loud clear voice attracting other people's attention to your situation. * Common peroneal nerve is located 4 to 6 inches above the knee. This strike causes motor dysfunction and a Charlie horse effect.

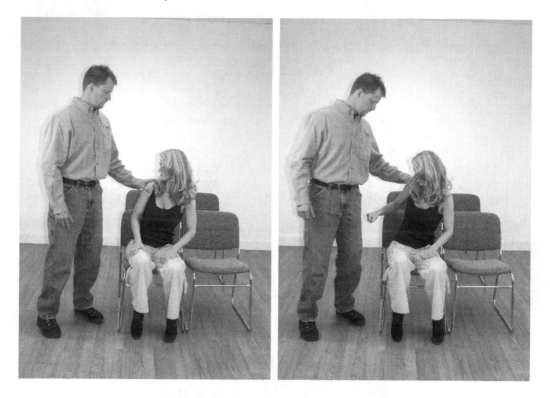

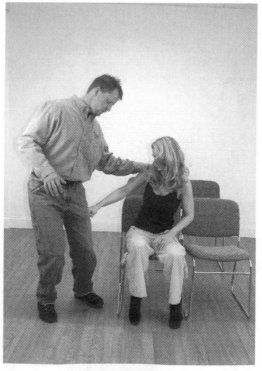

GRABBING YOUR BREAST – secure their hand tightly against your body. Grab one of their fingers and forcibly bend it backwards. Verbalize clearly, " Do not touch me again!"

NOTE: You could hyper extend the wrist in this position by holding tightly onto the finger and applying pressure to the finger as you lift the wrist upward. His palm will be facing up.

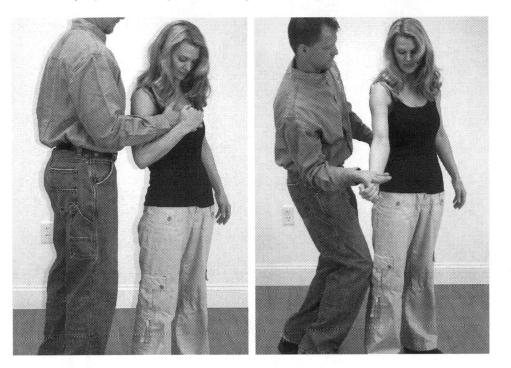

TOUCHED IN A SEXUAL MANNER ON YOUR REAR – hook onto their finger and forcibly bend it backwards. Verbalize clearly, " Do not touch me again!" OR break the finger if he threatened you.

NOTE: You could hyper extend the wrist in this position by holding tightly onto the finger and applying pressure to the finger as you lift the wrist upward.

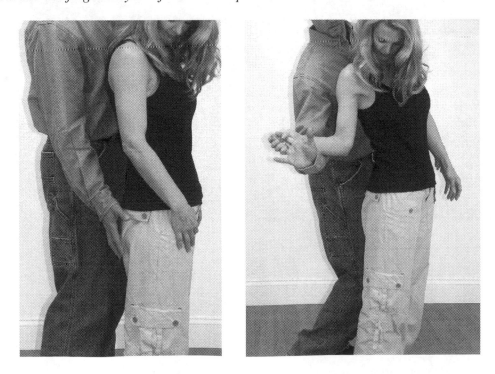

SITTING IN YOUR CAR, WINDOW ROLLED DOWN, SOMEONE GRABS YOUR ARM OR THROAT AND THREATENS YOU - With your right hand, finger jab into assailant's eyes. OR Using your left hand hook onto one of his fingers and break by bending it backwards. Eye jab with your right hand.

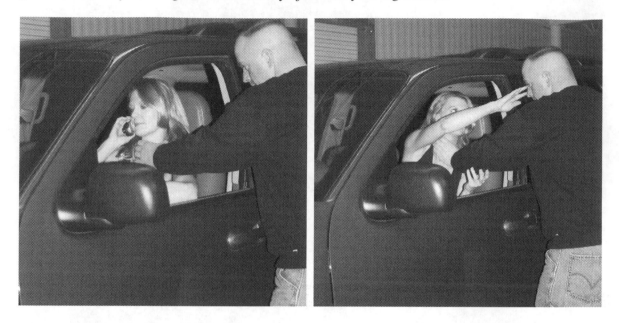

GRABBED FROM THE SIDE AS YOU ENTER YOUR CAR, YOU'RE NOT CARRYING PEPPER SPRAY - Eye jab or palm heel strike into the nose or side of his jaw. Punch or knee strike into the groin. Retreat to where you came from or get in your car from the other side; drive somewhere safe and report it.

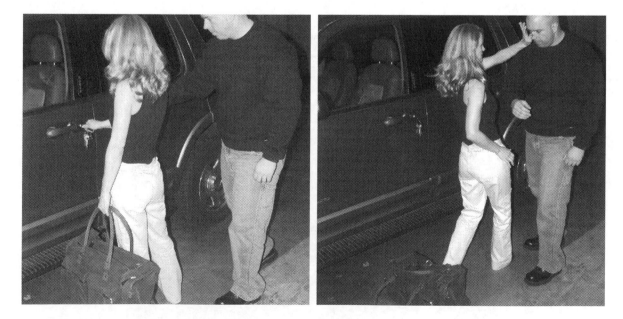

GRABBED FROM THE SIDE AS YOU'RE ENTERING YOUR CAR, YOU HAVE YOUR PEPPER SPRAY READY - Spray in a circular motion as you step to the side. Retreat to where you came from or get in your car from the other side; drive somewhere safe and report it.

ASSAILANT THROWING A PUNCH AT YOU – Deflect with your forearm, stepping out to the side but staying in close towards your assailant. Immediately eye jab with your blocking hand OR palm heel strike with the same hand you deflected with. Punch or knee strike into the groin.

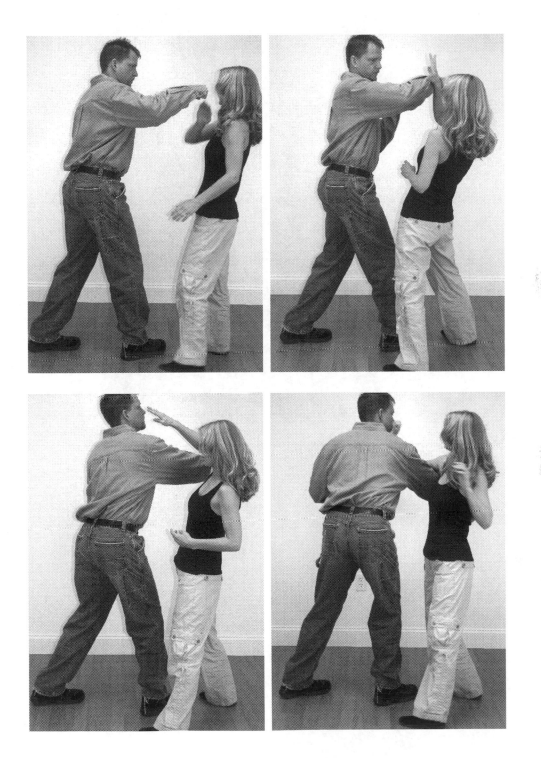

ASSAILANT THROWING A PUNCH AT YOU - Deflect and Hook onto the punching arm pull into you and knee strike.

DOUBLE HAMMER FIST STRIKE TO THE CHEST – one fist will be 6 inches directly above the other fist, (one on top the other with a 6 inch separation). You must twist your entire body into this strike. Have your hammer fist in position. Twist outwardly then with everything you've got, smoothly swinging them in front of your body, twisting both legs, pivoting on your feet, simultaneously twisting at your waist, turning your hips and turning your head to look at the chest of your assailant. The top hammer fist strikes between the breastbone (sternum) and the lower hammer fist will strike the abdomen, a few inches above the navel. You must visualize going through the chest. Do not stop on contact. This strike knocks the air out of him as well as shocking the system possibly causing him to pass out. Practice on a punching bag only.

Incorporate the techniques into your daily life. For instance, use an elbow strike to gently close the freezer door. Use your knee to close a drawer, use a low sidekick to close filing cabinets. Mentally role-play your techniques as you watch TV as a positive form of practice. When someone is threatened on a show, role-play the scene and tell yourself, "This is what I would do."

Be creative with the strikes that you will be learning and use them daily; use slow, controlled motion. Speed will come with time. You are training your mind to focus on the techniques at the same time locking your moves into your muscle memory. Learning slowly can mean learning more thoroughly.

Personalize the techniques that feel the most natural to you, and practice them repeatedly.

There is no one-size-fits-all approach to crime prevention. Just as there are no clear-cut answers for any situation. It's a judgment call. How willing you are to use it is up to you and you alone. Learn and practice the techniques with an open mind. Make it a habit by repetition; that way you will respond instinctively when under pressure of attack.

These techniques are suggestions only. A technique may work for one person but not for another, depending on your physique and physical abilities. You have to make the best decision for yourself.

Remember, Self-defense is being prepared for the unknown; it is defending oneself from attack or the threat of attack. Courage is the essence of self-defense.

And You've Got Courage!

SUGGESTIONS ON YOUR SELF-DEFENSE TRAINING:

- Learn a few techniques – practice them slowly, get comfortable with them then add a few more techniques. Do not try to learn all of the above techniques in two weeks.

- Relax and check your breathing. Do not hold your breath. Talk or yell at your (pretend) attacker.

- Control your vision, at first look at the chest not the eyes or hands. When striking focus your eyes on your target. Example; striking the knee look at the knee.

- Do not get frustrated - Speed will come with time.

- Do not allow this training to be something you learn today and gone tomorrow. Practice is key to making your strikes instinctive.

Statements I repeat during the 8-hour self-defense program:

- When you behave in an unexpected manner it disrupts his plan of action, it catches him off guard giving you that split second to retreat or strike.

- The one who strikes first usually wins. Be explosive.

- 1 – 2 – 3 strikes then retreat. The more strikes the better.

- Strike as soon as you're grabbed.

- Face your attacker – direct approach is best, strike hard and explosively.

- Strike the eyes, throat, groin and / or the knee.

- Don't be so fixated on what you are doing that you are unaware of what is going on around you. Criminals don't just appear out of nowhere! They appear from somewhere! Always be aware.

- Comply then surprise! (Attack)

- Think of your assailant as a target not a person.

- Strength against strength is ineffective it's your technique that counts.

- Do what you must to survive. Break all the rules.

- Violence must be met with violence.

- You are braver than you think!

Self-defense is not an automatic reflex nor is it instinctive. Self-defense must be learned.

COMMENTS FROM PARTICIPANTS THAT COMPLETED THE 8-HOUR PROGRAM:

The Self-Defense class offered by Sky was the best session I had ever attended on self- defense. Sky is not only outstanding in her field, but her instruction is very professional and credible. She cares about each student and makes sure that no one has missed a point and will repeat herself frequently to help concrete her points. I walked out of each session having more confidence because I knew how to handle myself or what I should do if I was ever in a pressing situation. My Mother and two of my sisters also took the course and we practice at home or give each other situations so we will always be ready to use them if need be. I would definitely recommend this class to all women for them to realize their worth and respect they deserve and will know how to stand up for themselves. This class changed certain aspects of how I view life and how I present myself and I am very thankful to my family for encouraging me to go. The information is priceless, yet it is up to each individual if it becomes knowledge.

GIVEN BY KATELYN - COLLEGE STUDENT

I attended the mother/daughter sessions with my adult step-daughter before she went on a solo vacation. She has a good head on her shoulders and can take care of herself, but I felt it important for her to attend and learn some additional skills "just in case". On her trip, she took along the door jam alarm and used it every night. Thankfully, her trip was a safe and fun one.

One of the things I found to be helpful in Sky's self-defense program was learning how to maneuver to get out of certain holds. I remember a neck hold where she showed me how my initial reaction would have caused me more bodily harm. She then proceeded to show a better way to break that hold. None of the moves were difficult – just not natural at first. It was very helpful to have time to practice them in class and get feedback on how we were executing the moves. I practiced at home and at work with the others from class. Thankfully, I haven't needed to use any of the moves we learned. The other tips and information has helped me be more thoughtful of my surroundings and I still think about possible defense and/or escape scenarios even if I do not actively practice the maneuvers.

GIVEN BY MICHELE T. - BUSINESS PROFESSIONAL.

I wish that self-defense classes such as yours had existed when I was my daughter Meg's age (13), and I wish more women like yourself were teaching our young women to be confident. Meg is, has always been, and will hopefully always be a very self-confident and strong young woman. She's never had body image issues, or problems with disliking herself, or with feeling like she's less important than anybody else.

I wanted to further improve her confidence by making certain that she is able to defend herself should the need ever arise. As her mother, of course I hope and pray that she will never need to use the skills you taught her, but knowing that she has those skills makes me sleep easier at night.

Meg's all I never was. I can't hide that I'm proud of her. She's unabashedly brave and she likes herself. She doesn't obtain her confidence by stepping on others or making others feel badly. One would think that a girl like Meg wouldn't need a class such as yours. But all girls do. Especially those who don't like themselves.

I like knowing that your program furthered her self-confidence, her ability to rely upon herself, and to know that she is worth defending.

Thank you, Sky for encouraging women of all ages and letting them know that feeling important is not selfish or greedy, or placing one above another. It's needed in order for a woman to be truly happy with herself, and her life.

GIVEN BY STACI B. - PROUD PARENT.

After taking the self-defense course, I came away feeling confident in knowing that I could protect myself from someone attacking me. Although I have never been in a situation where I have had to use self-defense. I have become more aware of my surroundings and have not put myself in a situation where I could be vulnerable to an attack. The self-defense program uses simple techniques that are easy to remember and can help one effectively get away from an attacker.

GIVEN BY SHEILA - HIGH SCHOOL STUDENT.

I would like to say that I carry the lessons that I learned from your classes with me all the time. I have become very observant and aware of my surroundings and the situations I am in all the time. I think twice before going places alone. I check my self-security.

I have also spoken to many acquaintances about the course and encouraged them to take self-defense awareness classes. It just makes sense.

GIVEN BY BARB F. - BUSINESS OWNER.

I feel like I have more confidence walking around in the mall (which I don't do often), street, ect... I am definitely more aware of my surroundings and I think to myself what would I do if different situations would occur. Thank you for the tips...I feel I am not naive anymore to the "weird" guys out there and I feel that I am ready to overcome a situation if it would arise (Hopefully I will never need to use my skills though). I have encouraged my friends to be aware of their surroundings also and have given them some tips. We, my family, have recommended your course to many people and feel that it is worth it. Thank you so much for the time and energy you spend for preparing for these classes!

GIVEN BY VALERIE T. - COLLEGE STUDENT

"Sky's Courage and Associates Self Defense Program has taught me that you need to project a confident aura around yourself even if you have had a horrible day. I am much more aware of my surroundings because Sky has taught me that even though there are awesome people in the world, there are people in so many places that could harm me. I am confident that I could defend myself in any circumstance if the situation called for it because of the knowledge I have gained in Sky's excellent Classes."

GIVEN BY LOREN D. - HIGH SCHOOL STUDENT

To contact Sky Armstrong for programs or personal appearances, visit www.getcourage.com.

Featured in the picture :

Julia A. / Crystal E. / Alicia F. / Loren D. / Richelle G. / Jacinda S. / Lisa S. / Michele T.

June K. / Megan B. / Staci B. / Jeanette S. / Taylor S. / Jordan S.

"In the eye of
the storm,
you will find
courage"

Sky Armstrong

Printed in the United States
By Bookmasters